YOU HAVE GOT TO BE KIDDING ME!

Breast Cancer Through a Husband's Eyes

GABE SABO

Cover designer's name: Marrianne Russell

ISBN: 978-1-6847-0909-0 (sc)
ISBN: 978-1-6847-0908-3 (e)

Library of Congress Control Number: 2019912784

Lulu Publishing Services rev. date: 10/30/2019

To Connie,
Your strength is incredible.

CONTENTS

INTRODUCTION

THERE ARE MOMENTS IN life that arrive out of nowhere and take you by surprise. I think God arranges these moments to help us on our journey. And in such moments, we are given an extra something that helps us make it through. Here is one of those times for me.

I can't recall exactly when this moment occurred, but it was sometime between my wife's first and second mastectomy and reconstruction. Connie was having some issues and we were at the doctor's three to four times a week. There was a lot going on in my head. Lord, why us? Where is the end to all this? Please heal Connie. How much more? Why, why, why? Maybe it was a pity party, I don't know.

I was at work at my job in retail. The position I held did not require me to work on the floor. I was in charge of processing the returns from customers. Most of my work was completed in the receiving department. On this particular day, I needed to go out on the floor and get some information about a product in the electrical department.

I had turned down the aisle to find what I needed when I noticed a couple shopping. As I was looking for the product, the husband looked up at me. I could see on his face that he was puzzled. His wife walked farther down the aisle. The man's expression changed. "Hey, I know you," he said. Now it was my turn to be puzzled. Looking at him, I did not recognize him at all. My brain struggled to figure out who he was.

"I've seen you at Dr. Donaldson's office in the waiting room," he said.

I still did not recall him. My thought was "Do you know how many times I have been there?"

"I remember you from the other day," he said.

I was still clueless.

"I was with my wife for her appointment and I saw you and your wife come out of the back from the exam rooms. You were checking out. My wife is going through breast cancer. Is your wife going through it, too?"

Shocked, I said nothing. Work was a place where I didn't have to deal with any cancer stuff. I kept very busy there so had no time to dwell on it. Now he had just uprooted my day. I had to think about it. "Yes," I replied, "she is battling it also."

"It was good for me to see another man there with his wife," he said.

My mind took off trying to recall all the appointments Connie and I had been to and whether there had been other men with the women in the waiting room. I could not remember many. Mostly, there had been two women together or a woman by herself.

The rest of our conversation was not very long. The whole encounter lasted five to ten minutes. We shook hands and looked at each other with a look that said, "Wow, someone understands what I am going through." He turned and walked to catch up with his wife.

I don't know how long I stood there watching them walk down the rest of the aisle. My mind was reeling from our short conversation. I had a lot to process.

As I look back on that day, I wished I had asked for his name and phone number. It happened so quickly and neither of us thought about that.

It was hard to work the rest of the day. Yes, he did uproot my day, but it was something I needed to know: I am not walking this alone. There are countless men walking the same walk, battling the same battle, and they, too, need to know they are not alone.

At this point, I would like to reference another book that could be beneficial to your reading experience: *The Courage to Be Imperfect*, written by my wife, Connie Sabo. There are details of her life in what she referred to as B.G. (before Gabe). Reading her book could enrich your understanding of my book and enable you to experience both sides of our story.

I have written my book with raw emotion, letting you in on what I was feeling and going through at the time we journeyed through cancer. The title, *You Have Got to Be Kidding Me,* comes out of the fact that almost everything that could go wrong did. As one doctor put it, some side effects happen to only one in a million. Well, we were one of the ones.

I let a friend read the manuscript. I gave it to him at church, slipping the notebook under his arm and whispering in his ear, "Are you ready for this?"

Come on, turn the page and join me on my journey.

CHAPTER 1

Pastor Approved

ON SATURDAY, DECEMBER 12, 1992, I attended a singles Christmas party at my church. That was where I began to get to know Connie. I had noticed her in our Sunday school class but hadn't talked to her much. During the party, Pastor Jerry approached me and suggested I talk to a really good-looking woman who was there. I thought, here we go again with someone trying to play matchmaker. I had discovered being single that everyone and their brother tried to fix me up.

The pastor was referring to Connie. There she was, in a black leather skirt and sweater with fur around the collar. She looked breathtaking. Later in the evening, the pastor's wife, Kay, approached me about talking to Connie as well.

Everyone was now ready to eat, however, and I was one of the last people in line. Food was arranged buffet style so I got my food and went to sit down in the screened-in patio room where everyone else was. There was only one table left with two seats, so I sat beside the hostess of the party, Millie. I had gotten to know her over the past few years and she had become a good friend. The next thing I knew, Connie came over and asked me if the seat next to me was taken. I nearly freaked out! I didn't know what to do. I told myself, get a grip and breathe, just breathe. I was pretty much forced to talk with her.

At that time, I was extremely shy. Connie was very outgoing. She had no problem striking up a conversation with anyone. During our conversation, I discovered Connie and I had a lot more in common than I thought: we were both from the same state, lived about two and a half hours apart, and had a lot of the same interests. I surprised myself by how well I did in talking with her. Before I knew it, dinner was over, so we started to clean up.

Pastor Jerry walked over to me and suggested I invite Connie out for coffee afterward. I didn't do that. I had just come out of a long-distance relationship that ended in a broken engagement, so I did not feel ready to pursue another.

The day after the Christmas party, Connie invited the singles Sunday School class to her house for fellowship and leftovers. Most of the people in the class went and so did I. It was a lot of fun. I got to see Connie in her own environment. I had the opportunity to talk to her for a little bit while she was in the kitchen. I helped bring dishes from the kitchen to everyone. Connie had done the majority of the cooking for the party. I didn't stay long since it was close to Christmas and I still had some shopping to do.

Sunday, December 20, 1992, I finally got up the nerve to ask Connie out. We were walking down the hallway after Sunday school, heading into the sanctuary for the church service when I asked if she would like to go to lunch with me. I wasn't really expecting her to say yes because I felt she was way out of my league. When she said yes, panic 101 flooded in. What do I do now? Not expecting that response, I now had to decide where we'd go. Oh, by the way, right after this, I had to go on the platform and play the drums, as I was the drummer for the praise and worship band. I had to work to focus, but I managed to do alright. It was a good thing I knew all the songs well.

For our lunch, I decided on a Mexican restaurant in Boca Raton. We had a good time just talking and getting to know each other. I ordered a combo plate and Connie ordered a taco salad. She ate all of hers, the shell included. Since I was finished and hadn't eaten all of mine, she wanted to know if she could have it. Wow, was I impressed! I found a woman who liked to eat. I had always seen women barely eat when they were out with a guy. After lunch, we strolled on the beach and just continued talking. It turned out to be an absolutely wonderful day.

For a period of time after this, we saw each other sporadically. Though I really liked her, neither of us was ready to leap into anything serious, as we discovered that both of us had just come out of broken engagements. Whenever we felt like one of us was starting to get serious, we backed off a little and just took it slow. We became really close friends. At times we wanted to take it to the next level, but we waited, which was a wise decision. I know now that investing the time to really get to know each other is well worth the effort for a couple.

It amazed me what Connie could inspire me to do. She was an avid reader and suggested a few books she would like me to read if I was interested in doing so. I agreed, thinking that I would go buy them and read them when I could. I did that for the first book, but she bought me the second book and suggested that we read it together. Huh? I didn't know about that. She said, "Oh, come on, let's try it and if you don't like it we will stop, okay?"

When we read the book together, she would read a chapter out loud then I would read one. I was not the best reader in the world, but she did not care at all about that. She would help me with words I did not know. If I did not stop at periods or pause at commas, she would remind me, "You are running everything together." It gave me a lot of confidence. The books we read and discussed brought us closer; the friendship really blossomed.

One book in particular was *Search for Significance,* by Robert S. McGee. That book changed my life forever (thank you, Robert McGee).

It is about self-worth and has an accompanying workbook. We each had our own book and workbook. We'd then get together and discuss in detail what we read. We spent a massive amount of time talking through it; it was quite a process. This was something Connie enjoyed: deep conversation. She liked to get to the root of the issues: why, how come, what do you think that was about? Not just any answer would do for her.

For me, this was uncharted territory. Prior to this, I had not come to grips with a lot of issues in my life. Like a dog with a bone, she would not let go until we worked through those issues. I thought maybe she would forget. No way! At some point, she would bring the subject up again or propose the idea of us working in the book. Finally, I just adjusted to digging deeper and cleaning out the closet, so to speak. One of the greatest things Connie did for me was to see beyond my outer appearance, look inside me, and see something worth investing in. I loved that about her.

In March of 1992 in one of our conversations, Connie told me that at the age of sixteen she'd had Hodgkin's disease. I wasn't familiar with that, so she explained it to me. Connie was a registered nurse and made it clear that there was a chance she could get cancer again, even though it had been almost eighteen years since she'd had Hodgkin's disease. She seemed sure that it would not return, which was reassuring to me. I thought about it for a little bit and came to the conclusion that it was unlikely it would return. I was willing to pursue our relationship. We started dating more seriously about April or May of that year.

Sometime toward the end of June, Connie told me she had found a lump on her right breast. She didn't seem particularly worried about it. The only time I had dealt with cancer before this was with my grandfather. When I was around seven or eight, I lost him to stomach cancer. At the time, we lived in California and he lived in Pennsylvania. Beyond that, I had not had to deal with it. I did think about the "what if" scenario—could I handle it?

A few weeks later, she had a doctor's appointment. He wanted to get a biopsy of the lump. As the day of the biopsy got closer, we prayed about it and she didn't seem worried. Connie wanted to go by herself to get the procedure done.

There were a lot of "what ifs" going on in my mind. What if it was cancer. What would I do? How would I handle it? The only thing that kept it from overwhelming me was Connie's lack of worry. We were fairly confident that everything would be alright.

I remember the day of the results of the biopsy all too well. I had to be at work until I received a call from her. I was dealing with it the best I could. It was on my mind a lot. I tried not to think about it, so I kept really busy. It was difficult, as dealing with cancer was new territory for me.

It was around 2:00 p.m. when one of the guys at work came and told me Connie was in the parking lot wanting to speak to me. I walked out and saw her in her car. When she saw me, she immediately got out of the car, came up to me, and threw her arms around me. In a low voice, she whispered in my right ear, "It's cancer."

I was stunned. I did not know what to say, so I just held her. I was holding someone who'd just found out she had cancer again. This was not what I was expecting to hear at all. What do I do now? I thought and the world seemed to stop for a moment or two.

Thinking about it now as I write this, Connie had a tremendous amount of trust in me so early in our friendship/relationship. It blows me away that, with such a personal issue as this, she let me in. She felt safe with me. I was so stunned by the news that it took my breath away. I had such a massive array of emotions, fear, and uncertainty. I was scared and I did not know what to do except hold her tight.

I was not aware of how long I held her, but I eventually let her go and went in to talk to my boss to see if I could get the rest of the day off. I went back outside and told Connie I could leave for the day, so we drove back to her house. On the way, a multitude of thoughts ran through my mind. I knew I had developed feelings for her, and now this?

We sat and talked for hours. I could not believe how long we talked. I don't remember what time it was when I went home. That night and the following day, I did a lot of reflecting about everything that was happening. I knew how I felt about her, but I was also scared. I wasn't sure what to do.

One of the things I realized was there was hope that things could work out for us. Even though she was beautiful and I was attracted to her beauty, there was even more that I was drawn to. She had a wonderful heart, a gentle spirit, and a great relationship with Jesus Christ. These were the most important things to me in looking for someone. Good looks are only for the short term, but what's on the inside is there for the long haul. Connie had everything I was looking for in the long run. You just don't find that in everyone you meet. It's kind of like a diamond—the more you look at it and examine it, the more you see its beauty. Most diamonds have flaws, but their beauty overshadows the flaws. Connie wasn't perfect, but her inward and outward beauty overshadowed any flaws.

Now there was this void, the unknown, darkness where there is no light. I was willing to walk in the unknown and seize the prospect of something more with her. I realized that no matter what, I could not let her go through this alone because a true friend doesn't walk away.

Connie made doctors' appointments to get information on what the treatment would be. The course of action was to undergo a mastectomy with reconstruction. This totally rocked her world. She was not happy with the plan set forth by the doctors. I didn't understand much about mastectomies or what that entailed. Connie conveyed to me what was involved and what the options would be. After that explanation, I was rocked, too. I did the best I could to support her. She needed some time to cope with all of this.

When Connie had had radiation for the Hodgkin's disease at such a young age, it was concentrated from the abdominal area up to her neck. That stunted the growth of her upper body where she did not develop as she should have and she was self-conscious about it. And now this?

I was pondering a lot of things. What if our relationship developed into something more, could I come to grips with a mastectomy? There was also the possibility of what they called reconstruction. This was a matter of rebuilding the breast with an implant of skin and possibly muscle. As I was working through this in my mind, Connie said she had a different idea.

CHAPTER 2

Pittsburgh and Dr. Who?

CONNIE HAD THE IDEA to contact the doctors in Pittsburgh who had treated her when she went through Hodgkin's disease as a teenager. She wanted a second opinion because she was not thrilled with the treatment recommended by the doctors in Florida. She felt there were other treatments available besides mastectomy. One particular doctor in Pittsburgh was renowned for treating cancer successfully.

Amazingly enough, when she called his office, they remembered her, so she was able to speak with him directly. His opinion was to remove the mass without a mastectomy in the procedure called a lumpectomy. He needed to see her, however, to arrive at a final decision for her situation.

Connie needed some time to digest this recommendation, as it was not something to jump into lightly. She took about a week or so to reflect on the information she received and she spent a lot of quality time in prayer. She then decided to go to Pittsburgh. She made arrangements to stay with her family who lived in Ellwood City, an hour or so north of Pittsburgh. When we were discussing this, Connie asked if I would go with her. I was kind of shocked and momentarily speechless at the magnitude of the request, but I told her I would.

We began setting things in motion, arranging for time off work and making airline reservations. The plan was for her to go to Pittsburgh first for a couple of weeks for all the doctor visits. I would join her a few days before the surgery was scheduled to take place. I would fly back home the day after surgery. Connie had to stay for a few additional weeks to start radiation treatments. They would inform her of the details of the radiation such as where it would be concentrated, frequency of treatments, and the exact measurements. When she came back to Florida, the doctors would be able to continue what was started in Pittsburgh.

As the time grew closer for the Pittsburgh trip, I was getting a little nervous about the idea of meeting her family. The more I reflected on it, I realized I needed to be myself and not be concerned with impressing anyone. On the flip side of meeting her family, a few days before Connie's surgery, my uncle on my dad's side of the family was celebrating their fiftieth wedding anniversary. There was going to be a cookout at my dad's sister's house. Connie and I attended this celebration together. Connie ended up meeting not only my immediate family, but also the entire clan of aunts, uncles, and cousins. We had only been dating for a few months and the next thing you know we were meeting each other's family. Connie fit right in with my family.

The time came for me to drive her to the airport. We told each other goodbye and off she went to Ellwood City, Pennsylvania. She called after arriving to let me know everything went well. The next day or two she would travel down to Pittsburgh for the doctors' appointments. I was a bit nervous about what they would find and what their prognosis would be. I wondered if they would agree with the doctors in Florida or if they would stand by what they previously said concerning the possibility of just removing the mass without a mastectomy.

After a few appointments, they made their decision, saying they should be able to remove the mass without any problems and follow that up with radiation. Connie and I were quite relieved and thrilled with this prognosis. After this report, I hopped on a plane and headed to Pittsburgh.

The first person I met was Mark, Connie's younger brother. We ate at a little place called the Hot Dog Shop, which was one of Connie's favorite places to eat. We then drove to their parent's house where I met the rest of the family. Everyone was very nice and it reminded me somewhat of my own family. I was glad to get our meeting "out of the way," so I could focus more on the reason we were there. The surgery was scheduled for the next morning at 9:00, which meant we had to be at the hospital in Pittsburgh at 6:00 a.m. I drove Connie there. Her parents came at 8:30 a.m. This would be the first of many times I would be at the hospital with Connie.

When it was time for Connie to go to surgery, we all said our goodbyes as the hospital staff took her away on a gurney. We went to the waiting room and camped out there until her surgery was finished. It was pleasant to sit and talk to her parents, as they were down-to-earth people. It was helpful for me to have others with me, as it made the time go by quickly and kept my mind busy so I wouldn't think too much.

After a couple of hours, the doctor came in to discuss how the surgery had gone. He said everything went really well and they were able to get all the cancer. All of us heaved a big sigh of relief. He also said that she was in the recovery room and would be in there for a little while before she could go home. That startled us, as we didn't think Connie would be able to go home that quickly. We thanked him very much for everything.

I don't remember how much time elapsed before we were told that we could go back and see her in the recovery room. When we saw her, she looked well for having just gone through surgery. She was still a little groggy from the anesthesia. We were able to talk to her, but she faded in and out on us. The nurses said it would be a little while before she was able to leave, so her parents decided to go back home. They asked if Connie and I would be okay. We said we'd be fine, so they left.

In an hour or so, the nurse notified me that Connie could be discharged.

She gave me instructions on where to bring the car so I could pick her up. She brought Connie out in a wheelchair and helped her get into the car. Connie said she knew how to get home from Pittsburgh because she remembered traveling to this hospital every day with her family when she was young. So away we went.

Connie was awake with me for about five minutes. The next thing I knew she was out cold, sleeping soundly. I tried to get her to wake up, but that didn't work. Suddenly, it hit me that I was driving in downtown Pittsburgh and didn't know it well. I had previously lived south of Pittsburgh but never went downtown. I was heading to Connie's house not knowing where I was going. I was freaking out being on my own to figure out how to get there. At that time, we didn't have a cell phone. Well, it wouldn't do me any good anyway to have a cell phone because I didn't know her parent's phone number or address. It was only by the grace of God that I finally found Route 79, which I knew was the route we had taken on our way to the hospital. So I headed north.

Connie would wake up once in a while, mumble a few things and doze back off to sleep. In my mind, I was trying to retrace my steps to her house. I drove for quite a while and then recognized the exit from the trip earlier that day. Once I got off the exit, I just started heading in the direction I thought I should go. In my mind, I thought, "Oh great! I am out in the middle of nowhere trying to find a place that I have only been to once, and my copilot is sleeping." I thought to myself, this is not even funny. I can't even stop and ask for directions because I don't know addresses, phone numbers, or anything. I just kept driving. Finally, I started seeing landmarks that looked familiar. I couldn't believe that I actually drove straight to her house without making any wrong turns.

We got Connie in the house and settled in. Most of the evening she was still in and out of it. The next day my plane was scheduled to leave around 2:00 p.m. I needed to drop off my rental car at the airport. Connie's parents got in their car and guided me to Route 79 from a different route than I had traveled before. Connie rode with me until we got to the exit where I would have to turn. We said goodbye and I headed to the airport. Connie rode back home with her parents.

I was familiar with the old airport from when I lived there. Since that time, a brand new airport had been built. I figured I could find the rental car place and return the car. When I got there, I couldn't find it; I looked everywhere. I asked one of the attendants where it was and he told me it was at the old airport. Oh, great! Here I arrive at the new airport only to be told I now have to travel to the old airport then get shuttled back to the new airport for my flight. So I got directions and took off. I found the old airport, but guess what? No car rental place. It was one o'clock and I just knew I was going to miss my flight.

The only thing I could think to do was go back to the new airport and leave the car in the parking lot. When I got back to Florida, I'd call Connie and ask her to return the car for me. I couldn't miss my flight because I had to be back to work the following day. I called Connie when I returned home and told her what happened. She and her dad went to the airport the next day and returned the car.

I raced into the airport and barely made my flight. It was a two-hour trip back to Florida, so I had some time to reflect about everything that had happened during this trip. I knew I wouldn't see Connie for two to three weeks. I thought it would be good for us to have a little bit of distance from each other since we spent so much time together in Florida. I thought it would be a good opportunity to see how much I would miss her and evaluate my feelings toward her. This would actually be the first time since we had started dating that we would be apart for a period of time.

We talked on the phone; it was on the landline. It was good; it just wasn't the same as being with her. As the weeks went on, I realized I really did miss her and being around her. I missed our conversations. She brought out more things in me than I had realized.

Before I met Connie, I was a quiet and reserved person. I was shy and also very passive. I didn't defend myself and basically let people run over me. I started changing a little bit before I met Connie, but she challenged me in different ways. She was very outgoing, confident, and social. I wasn't. She would ask me a lot of questions, which would probe my mind and make me think about different things in my life. I realized I missed that. I liked the change that was going on inside me. A lot of people didn't care for that change, but I guess that's to be expected when you were the way I was.

In addition to phone calls here and there, we had the good old-fashioned US postal service, sending cards and notes to each other. About two weeks went by and I finally received the phone call from Connie saying she was heading back to Florida. The doctors had done everything they could do up there, so they told her she could follow up with radiation treatments in Florida.

I knew Connie was very excited to get back to Florida just to be home in her own house again. She asked if I would pick her up at the airport. Of course I would. On the way there, I stopped and got some flowers for her. She came off the plane, looking great. I surely did miss her.

We saw a lot of each other the next few weeks. We had a lot to talk about. We discussed things that happened during the doctor visits and about the time she spent with her family. It was not the same when she came back; we both saw things in a different way after going through this. Our perspectives had changed. Seeing the way she interacted with her family and their relationship was beneficial for me. A great deal can be learned from the way you treat your family. If you treat your family well, then more than likely, you will treat other people well, too.

In the proceeding weeks, Connie began radiation treatments on the side where they performed the lumpectomy. She got through them fairly well. She was a little fatigued on the days with the radiation treatments. There was some time between treatments when she had a little more energy. We spent a huge amount of time together. My feelings for her were growing daily. The more time we spent together the more those feelings deepened. A year and a half later, we decided to get married.

14

CHAPTER 3

Our Wedding

WE BEGAN DISCUSSING MARRIAGE in December 1994, as we knew we wanted to spend the rest of our lives together. We fit so well together as a couple that it was like being married already. Without even realizing it, we had worked on our relationship to get it to this point. Even though we had our own places to live, I spent most of my time at Connie's house. She rented a house and I had a small apartment. We did not live together because we wanted to do this right. It was very hard for me to go home every night. We planned a quiet evening at Connie's house cooking dinner together and just hanging out spending time with each other.

After dinner that night, we were talking and I asked Connie if she would marry me. Her immediate response was yes. I did not have a ring at the time I proposed because I had learned in previous conversations when we were discussing marriage that she wanted to have one custom made. We looked at various rings in the jewelry stores to no avail. Connie had exquisite and lavish taste. There was a jeweler in our church so we made an appointment to meet with him to have a ring custom made for Connie.

We were paying for the wedding so it would be whatever Connie wanted. When Connie dropped the bombshell on me of who, what, where, and when, I asked if she was serious. She was indeed! Wow! It took me a little while to grasp the grandness of it all.

We made the decision to have the wedding at the Breakers Hotel in Palm Beach in the Mediterranean courtyard. The reception was held in one of the hotel ballrooms. Connie wanted the reception to be a cocktail wedding reception with no tables. She wanted chairs set around the room in semi-circles so people would have to mingle. She didn't want people just to stay at their tables. She wanted everyone to have fun and socialize.

She got a custom-made wedding dress. She did not want the traditional music or organ music as she walked down the aisle. She wanted to walk down the aisle to Rachmaninoff, played by a harpist, a violinist, a bassist, and a flutist.

We set the date of the wedding for July 15 at 6:00 p.m. There were four in the wedding party. The maid of honor was Connie's sister, Nancy. The bridesmaids were my sisters, Rose and Kathy, along with Connie's best friend, Karen. The best man was my brother-in-law Barry and the groomsmen were Connie's brothers, Mark and Rick, along with my very best friend, Mike (who is known as Spike).

The center of the courtyard had a sunken area with a pond surrounded by an ornate decorative wall. The ceremony was held there. The bridesmaids were dressed in long black evening gowns with elbow-length black gloves. They each carried a single white rose entwined with ivy. They entered the courtyard through a French door and walked through the guests who were seated on the terrace, which was lined with ferns and topiaries. It was two or three steps down to where we were waiting. As the ladies entered, I looked around for a second or two. There were a few people inside the hotel watching from the windows. Once all the bridesmaids arrived, the French doors were closed. After a few moments the doors opened revealing Connie on the arm of her father, Loren.

Connie's dress was form-fitting with a massive amount of beadwork on it along with lace and a long train. She had a headpiece with lace down the back. There was no veil around her face. Her bouquet was white roses with baby's breath.

I saw Connie standing there in the doorway; she was so beautiful. The sight of her took my breath away. The smile on her face was worth it all. I remember us locking eyes for a moment. It was as if time stood still. It is a memory I will never forget. The old saying that the wedding day is the bride's day is true. Connie was the center of attention, as her father escorted her down the aisle; all eyes were fixed on her.

We did not use the traditional wedding vows. We used vows from the wedding of one of Connie's cousins that we had attended. When we heard them, we loved them. Before I knew it, we were pronounced husband and wife. The ceremony had gone smoothly. I had waited a very long time for this moment. I was truly the most blessed man on earth. Connie was so worth the wait. I married my best friend; I was so honored.

Connie also wanted a bridal dance. When she told her father that, he freaked out because he had never danced before. She gave him plenty of time to practice. There was no way he was getting out of it. It was a real joy to see them dance together.

The food was delicious and the cake was awesome. We chose to go with finger foods instead of the traditional meal. Our photographer was Ken from our church. A few weeks before the wedding, he took Connie and one of her friends on a private photo shoot at an old Palm Beach church, Bethesda by the Sea. This was his wedding gift to us and those photos are some of my favorites.

We stayed at the Breakers Hotel the night of our wedding. The following day we returned to Connie's house in the West Palm Beach area. We stayed home for a few days to see everyone and say goodbye as they all went back to their home states. It was so much fun to have our families around us. After everyone left, we had a few days remaining in the week, so we arranged to go to Amelia Island, Florida, for the rest of the week. We stayed at a bed-and-breakfast. Our room had a covered deck from which we could step right onto the beach. We spent a lot of time on the beach, as well as going downtown to wander around and take photos; it was a quaint place.

We did not know it yet, but there was a mix-up in our reservation checkout date. We got up Saturday morning and spent some time on the beach and then went downtown to get something to eat. When we arrived back at our room, there was a note on the door for us to go to the front desk for a very important message. There, they informed us that we were not booked that night. While we were at lunch, they had packed up all of our belongings and had them waiting for us in a small room next to the desk. We argued with them to no avail. They had no other rooms available and the only place on the island to stay was at the country club for $400 a night. That was not in the budget.

We had no choice but to get in our red Explorer and make our way to Interstate 95 heading north to Asheville, North Carolina where we would spend the next week. We were unable to clean up for our trip, which would be a six- or seven-hour drive. At this point, it was about one in the afternoon. We called the bed-and-breakfast in Asheville where we were to stay to find out if we could check in early, but we could not. Upon arriving in Asheville, we stopped at a few hotels, but they were all booked solid. Well, as you can guess, there were no rooms available in Asheville. We talked to one of the clerks at the desk of one the hotels where we stopped and they said they tried most of the hotels and motels in the area and they were all booked for the night.

We found a lead on a hotel on the east side of town that might have some rooms, so we quickly traveled to it. It was a very small, old-looking place. When we entered our room, we noticed it was not the cleanest place we'd ever stayed. The furniture did not match and Connie was not thrilled about it at all. We were exhausted, so we stayed. Being the nurse that she was, Connie had rubbing alcohol in one of the bags and she wiped down the entire bathroom. She would not let me walk barefoot on the carpet because of how dirty it was. She suggested I wear flip-flops. She pulled the comforter back on the bed to check to see if the sheets were okay to sleep on. She even had me prop a chair under the door handle so to make sure no one would enter.

We made the best of it, knowing the next day we could actually be in the bed-and-breakfast we originally planned on. What a night it was, happy honeymoon to us!

The next day we were excited to arrive at the Colby House Bed and Breakfast. It was a yellow two-story house with white trim and a wraparound porch. The couple who owned it was from South Florida. They had retired to Asheville and wanted to run a bed-and-breakfast. The house was furnished with beautiful furnishings they had brought with them from Florida. The breakfasts were mouth-watering, as the owner's wife did all the cooking. I remember one morning we had French toast that was made using orange juice. It was wonderful. By the end of the week, there were just two couples staying there. The owner's wife would ask us what we wanted for breakfast. She began to name items, but it was too much to choose from. We ate well.

We stayed a week in Asheville, sightseeing, taking photos, shopping, and exploring. We had a fabulous time for the rest of the week. At the bed-and-breakfast, we met some wonderful people from Florida. They lived not far from where we lived and we became good friends with them after we returned home. One of the couples we met there were Bill and Georgie. We went to dinner a few times and had breakfast together every morning with them. They were in Asheville attending a conference at the Cove, Billy Graham's Conference Center in Black Mountain.

Our room in the bed-and-breakfast did not have a bathroom in the room; it was across the hall. This is what I will never forget: One morning Connie was in the bathroom getting ready for the day and I needed something from the bathroom, so I knocked and Connie let me in. I got what I needed and left, when Bill saw me. He pulled me aside and said that is one the greatest things you can do for your marriage. He had my attention so he went on and said it is to spend time with your wife in the bathroom when she is getting ready, putting on her makeup and doing her hair. He said take the time to sit and talk to her, as this would be a very wise investment. "Georgie and I have been married over twenty years and I never stopped going in there with her," he said.

I continued spending time in the bathroom with Connie after that; it was quality time spent with her. The conversations we had were meaningful. Bill was right, an investment it truly was.

Soon it was time to return to West Palm Beach.

CHAPTER 4

Married Life

WE ARRIVED BACK IN West Palm Beach to start life as a married couple. We both had to go back to work the following Monday. At the time, I worked a steady day job from seven to five at a lumber company not far from where we lived. The company had a fleet of seventy-five vehicles consisting of about five company cars, three full-size pickup trucks, three or four tractor-trailers that were flatbed trailers used for hauling roof trusses they made, four flatbed trucks used to haul steel rebar which is used in concrete to make it stronger, and the remaining vehicles were twenty-one-foot flatbeds with dumping abilities, which hauled lumber to the job sites. I was hired to do all the bodywork and painting on the trucks and cars. We also had a mechanic shop with four full-time mechanics to fix the vehicles when they broke down or needed maintenance.

I worked there a few years before I met Connie. Once the managers discovered I was also a mechanic, it was not long before I was given the responsibility of mechanics, bodywork and painting. Additionally, I drove the tandem tow truck that the company owned to retrieve their broken trucks or pull trucks out when they got stuck in the sand.

Connie was a nurse and worked in the intensive care unit at the hospital. Her schedule was the 7 p.m. to 7 a.m. shift four nights a week. Connie started her nursing career in South Florida. She was employed by a couple of hospitals and a vascular surgeon who specialized in trauma, along with being the director of the county paramedics. She assisted the vascular surgeon with surgeries in addition to making field runs with him and the paramedics. (For more about Connie's nursing career, see the chapter "My Search for Meaning" in her book, *The Courage to Be Imperfect*.) She liked this job with the vascular surgeon more than others, but he quit his practice and closed the office so Connie went back into the hospital system.

We continued to be active in our church. I continuously played the drums and was involved with the church's evangelism team. Connie wanted to help me with the team, but it was difficult for her to participate due to working night shifts and weekends.

Connie loved the arts; she earned an associate degree in art history from a local college. In one of the classes, she worked on painting. One particular painting she did was a reproduction of Picasso's *Woman in Blue;* it was incredible. She also took photography classes there. She was a very good photographer. Her specialty was black-and-white photos. She had a very keen eye as to whether the subject would look good in black and white.

I also liked photography before I met Connie, so we had that in common as well. When I lived in Pennsylvania before moving to Florida, my dad owned a 35mm camera, which I used to take a lot of pictures. I did not understand all the settings on the camera, but I liked photography. Connie bought me my first 35mm camera a year before we were married; it was a Minolta that was all manual. Back then you had to adjust the f-stops and shutter speeds to take good pictures. Connie taught me a lot about photography and this became a passion for both of us.

We enjoyed taking photos together, so we took a lot of weekend trips to different places in South Florida to capture moments. There are two places in particular we went a lot and never get tired of taking photos there. One was St. Augustine and the other was Vizcaya, Miami. We made many trips to St. Augustine around Easter and Thanksgiving. In the center of town, there was an art festival those holiday weekends. We stayed at a bed-and-breakfast in town. By staying there, you could easily get to everything you wanted to see. We loved walking around the festival and town taking photos.

Vizcaya is another wonderful place; it belonged to John Deering who started International Harvester Company. His mansion now belongs to Dade County. His house is an Italian style villa with gardens that sits right on the Intercostal. We spent most of our time wandering around the gardens taking a ton of photos. The inside of the house is very nice with all its antiques and paintings. The atmosphere of the house and its beauty were spectacular. Connie also introduced me to opera, ballet, and smooth jazz music. In the late 1990s, the Kravis Center for the Performing Arts opened in West Palm Beach, Florida. I never thought in one million years that I would ever like going to see an opera or a ballet. The first opera we saw was *The Magic Flute.* It is on the lighter side and easy to follow. A ballet we saw together was *Sleeping Beauty.* Something unimaginable happened that night during the intermission. Connie wore a bright-blue, long-sleeved, wrap-around turtleneck dress. The bottom of the dress from above the knee had long fringes that hung down to the ankle. The hemline of the fringes went from the top of the right knee and down at an angle toward the left hip. She looked beautiful in that dress. At intermission, we went to the lobby and a woman in her early thirties asked Connie if she was one of the dancers. Connie was shocked to be asked that question. She replied no and asked why the woman thought that. The woman said she saw a lot of ballets and was sure Connie was in the ballet by the way she walked and carried herself. Connie thanked her for her comment. We talked about that for a long time!

We saw the Three Tenors in Miami at Joe Robbie Stadium. We took my mom with us because she loved the opera, too. It was impressive how those men could sing! The power of their voices is astonishing. Out of everything we attended, the most memorable experience for both of us was when we were able to see Pavarotti on Miami Beach. They set the entire stage right on the beach. Plywood was laid down for the chairs to be put on the stage and all the lights as well. It was far enough away from the ocean that there were no issues with the water. It was early spring, so the weather was cool but not cold. The concert started right at sunset. As the sun was setting and the ocean waves were crashing with a light breeze blowing, Pavarotti was singing. If this is anything of what heaven will be like, it will be tremendous.

As I write this, almost twelve years later, I am in a coffee shop looking out the window. My mind was there on Miami Beach. I think I can almost feel and hear the ocean. It was an experience I will never forget. I think it was the setting and the atmosphere of it all that were phenomenal. We found the ticket stubs from the concert and the newspaper clippings we kept from the *Miami Herald.* Approximately 120,000 people attended Pavarotti's concert that evening. My thought was we were two of 120,000 people that were able to see and hear Pavarotti on the beach.

Connie also introduced me to art museums and we attended quite a few. One in particular was the Norton Museum of Art in West Palm Beach. One of the exhibits they sponsored was Andrew Wyeth's Helga Pictures, a series of watercolors he did of a neighbor. One of the greatest things of all was that I had Connie as a commentator and guide; she was in her element. Like a child in a candy store, she did not know which way to go first. I don't remember how long we were there, but it was a long time. It's not very often that this type of showing comes around, so you better enjoy it while you are there and we did. I remember turning left in the gallery and going around a corner. At the opposite end of the hallway was a picture of Helga in a winter coat called *The Prussian,* the painting made us stop in our tracks and stand in awe. It looked like she was actually standing at the end of that hallway. Once we arrived at the painting and looked at the particular features, it was remarkable. I remember the detail of one of the coat buttons that was so real, you could not tell it was painted. What a day it was, the time spent with Connie, the memories we had—that is what life is all about.

We also loved fishing. My parents lived in a housing development with a lake behind the house. We would go bass fishing there. My sister Kathy and her husband, Barry, also loved to fish. They would join us in fishing for hours; we had so much fun.

Another sport we loved was rollerblading. We did this for quite a few years until the doctors would not let Connie skate anymore due to them not wanting her to fall and break any bones.

Here's a story I just thought of as I wrote this. It happened while Connie and I were dating. Before I met her, I had a 1975 Corvette Stingray that I bought in 1982 while I was living in Pennsylvania. A friend of mine went with me on a road trip to South Florida to visit my sister Rose. While we were there, my dad became ill and we had to fly home to Pennsylvania, so I had to leave the car in Florida. It was hard to do that, to leave it, but I had no choice. There was no garage to store it, so it had to sit out in the sun and the sun in the South Florida destroyed the paint by fading and cracking it.

A year or two later we moved from Pennsylvania to South Florida. The car sat for many years before I could restore it. I started the restoration process of the car before I met Connie. The car was at my parent's house in the garage and I knew they were going to sell their house, so it had to be finished before they put the house on the market. I had most of the bodywork completed except for the primer, paint, and interior of the car. I worked most Saturdays on it. The Saturdays Connie did not work she said she wanted to help me on the car. I was shocked that she wanted to; I knew she liked to do projects around the house, but this was a car. She would have to deal with bodywork, dirt, dust, and paint fumes. But she wanted to help, so I told her she could meet me at my parent's house early Saturday morning. That time was difficult for her because she was not an early morning person. I wanted to get started before it got too hot outside to work. Connie arrived in the late morning. That particular day, we were going to do the final sanding on the car so I could paint it.

The final sanding consisted of 1200 grit wet/dry sandpaper on a sanding block and water. The sanding block is used to make the sure the primer is sanded smooth and there are no high or low spots in it. There is no dust, which makes the sanding easier. Connie arrived with her blonde hair in a ponytail. She wore black running shorts, a t-shirt, flip-flops, and sunglasses and had a cup of coffee in her hand. I was already sanding when she said she was ready and asked what she needed to do. She told me not to give her things to do just to keep her busy because she really wanted to help. I looked at her and just chuckled to myself. I gave her sanding-block sandpaper and a bucket of water, and then showed her how to do it. Her reply was "I know how to use sandpaper, so I think I can manage." Okay, I told her if she had any questions to ask me. I went back to my side of the car and continued to sand. Connie started on the right side of the car on the rear fender.

About ten minutes later, I heard "Gabe, can you come check this? I'm done."

I said I'd be there in a second. Now, mind you, I'd been working on the rear fender on my side of the car for over twenty minutes to get it level, and Connie was done in ten minutes? I went to her side of the car, looked, and told her she needed to keep sanding. I showed her what she needed to do to get it level. I went back to my side of the car and continued to sand. I could hear sanding away, and then about 15 minutes later, I heard, "Can you come check this?"

Again, I looked, and then told her no, not yet, keep sanding. I don't remember how long this went on, but it was a while. Finally, I heard, "Can you come check this?"

This time it looked good. "You're done and you can move now to the door," I said.

"Do you know how long it has taken me to do this?" she replied. "We are going to be here all day!"

"Yes, I know it took you a long time and thank you, but yes, we will be here most the day. It has to be precise, so the car will look good after it's painted."

She said alright. It did take most of the day; it was an enjoyable day with Connie. We talked throughout and took a lot of breaks.

I scheduled to paint the car the following Saturday. I rented a paint booth to spray the car in. Connie asked if she could go with me because she was interested in knowing the whole process of painting the car. She wanted to be in the spray booth with me. I was excited that she wanted to be part of this. I told her she needed to be at my parent's house early in the morning so we could get to the booth and get started before it got too hot.

The following Saturday, Connie arrived on time. I told her before she came to make sure she wore old clothes, long sleeves, and put her hair up so she could wear a paint hood that would keep the paint out of her hair. We were ready to go and I could see she had on flip-flops. I asked her if she'd brought any other shoes. No was her reply. I told her she might want to get different shoes because there will be blue paint in the air. "I'll be alright," she said. I told her we could stop by her house on the way there and she could get some other shoes to wear. "No, I don't need shoes," she replied. Can you see where this is going? "Okay," I said, "let's go."

We did get the car painted that day and it looked brand new. It came out better than I anticipated. Once we got there. I forgot about the flip-flops because there was so much to do with the car. We put the car back on the trailer, so we could return to my parent's house, delivering the car to their garage. At some point, I looked down at Connie's feet and they were bright blue like the Smurfs.

"You might want to look at your feet," I said.

She did and exclaimed, "They're blue!"

This is where I had to choose my words wisely. "That's why I suggested we stop by your house and get some shoes," I said.

"What are you going to do about this?" she replied.

What was *I* going to do about it?

"It was your car and I was helping you," she said.

I just shook my head, went and got some paint thinner and some rags. I ended up cleaning the blue paint off Connie's feet the best I could.

After being in Florida for a while something on the inside of both of us wanted a simpler life, so we started to look into Asheville, North Carolina.

CHAPTER 5

Where in the World is Asheville?

At separate times in our lives, we both had a desire to visit Asheville, North Carolina. We were fond of the mountains and scenery. We were both ready to get away from the big city and into what we thought at the time would be a simpler life.

After three years of being married, the doors finally opened for us to relocate to Asheville. We made another trip in the fall to Asheville for a long weekend, met with the real estate agent, and looked at three or four houses that weekend. We also looked at bigger houses that possibly could be converted into a bed-and-breakfast, and looked at old houses that needed work—fixer-uppers. We looked at established bed-and-breakfasts that were for sale, but they were out of our price range.

On our last afternoon, the real estate agent said there was one more house on the west side of town that she wanted to show us. It was a smaller three-bedroom house with a basement that needed a little work but nothing major. It was in the last stages of foreclosure and the agent didn't know if we could even put a bid on the house. After a few phone calls, we put a bid on it and the bank accepted our offer.

All the parts to buying the house and moving were quite an endeavor. I look back now and wonder, what in the world were we thinking? We acquired a loan for a house with no jobs in a different state from where we lived—that it worked just had to be God.

We arranged everything for the move. We rented a truck and put one car on a trailer behind the truck, which I drove. Connie drove the Explorer and towed her car behind that. The game plan was to depart early Wednesday morning and drive straight through, which would probably take us twelve to thirteen hours. My sister Rose would drive down from Virginia and meet us there. My mom traveled with us.

The closing of our house was scheduled for Friday and we thought we could get everything painted late Friday evening. Saturday we could finish any touch-up work or finish any painting we might not have been able to complete on Friday, and then begin moving everything in. My mom and I were going to leave Sunday and head back to Florida because I had to work another week of the two-week notice I gave at my job. Connie was going to stay in Asheville and settle in.

We got the truck packed up, loaded all the cars, and tried to get some sleep, as we were going to leave around 4:00 a.m. We didn't end up leaving until 9:00 a.m. We traveled for a while, got to Jacksonville, Florida, and pulled into a rest stop. Every time we stopped, I made a point of checking the truck and trailers to ensure everything was alright. I noticed on the vehicle trailer Connie was pulling that one of the straps that held the car on the trailer had broken. I had to call the rental company to have the strap fixed, which took about two hours.

We got back on the road and continued heading north. We reached South Carolina at 2:00 a.m. It took forever for us to get that far. We were extremely tired, so we decided to pull into a rest stop and sleep for a little while before resuming our trip. We slept about two hours, got up, and took off again.

When we were heading back onto the highway, I could see smoke coming from the trailer I was pulling. Connie was behind me flashing and blinking her lights to get my attention. I pulled over, got the flashlight out, looked at the trailer, and saw one of the tires had blown. At that point, I'd had enough. Here we were on the side of the road, in the middle of the night, with a flat tire.

I got back into the truck, called the rental truck place, and explained the situation to them. They would have someone out as soon as possible. I was really frustrated and getting angry because things weren't cooperating with our plan. I knew approximately where we were and how long it would take for us to get to Asheville. It didn't look like we were going to make the closing on the house.

It was two hours before the mechanic showed up. When he arrived, it was really late in the morning. He was going to put on a tire. When he got the tire off, he discovered there was more than just a flat tire. It looked like the brakes on the trailer had locked up and burned up everything, which caused the tire to blow. From my background in the automotive field, I knew we were in trouble. He made a phone call and the only option available was to get another trailer. The only problem was that the closest trailer was in Augusta, Georgia. They couldn't have it to us until after 1:00 p.m. the next day.

I had a million things funneling through my mind, like what if we missed our closing? How are we going to get moved in? My mom and sister could only be there for the weekend, so if we missed the closing on Friday, we couldn't close on the house until the following week and they wouldn't be available to help us. I knew I had to get a grip on this, so I took a few seconds to say a quick prayer, then fill in Connie with the details (the rental company would put us up in a hotel room for the night and the new trailer would arrive the following day). There was nothing else we could do.

The mechanic was finally able to free up the brakes and put on a new tire. We headed north once again and followed him to the hotel at the next exit. We got settled in the room and tried to go to sleep. I lay there for a while with a whirlwind of scenarios about closing on the house and moving in running through my brain. We wanted to paint the house before we moved in, but I knew that was not a reality. I couldn't stand to think about it anymore, so I tried to put it out of my mind. Eventually, I drifted off to sleep.

The next morning, we had to call the real estate agent and explain the situation. We told her we would not arrive until later that evening and would miss the closing. After a series of phone calls back and forth, they postponed the closing until Monday.

The rental company arrived with the trailer at 1:00 p.m. We had to unload the car, unhook the trailer, hook up the new trailer, and reload the car. We got back on the road and I knew we had five to six hours of driving ahead of us, so I had a lot of time to reflect on the events that were taking place. It was scary moving to a new area, besides the fact that we had missed the closing on our house. Here we were driving with everything we owned in the truck and we had no place to go. I said a lot of prayers in the hours that followed.

When we arrived at the North Carolina border, we had to drive up a mountain that was unbelievably long and steep. About halfway up the mountain, the truck started to slow down. At the three-quarter mark, the truck almost came to a complete stop. I was in the far right lane of the road. Connie was behind me with the flashers on. Tractor trailers were passing me uphill; I wasn't even going five miles an hour. I didn't think we would make it. I had my foot on the gas pedal and it was pressed all the way down to the floor. The truck was an automatic, so I put it in the lowest gear. It seemed like it took us forever to get up that mountain and to our hotel.

We checked in and just waited for my sister to arrive. She had called a little bit earlier to say she was about an hour away. Once my sister arrived, the real estate agent said we could meet her at the house to see what we needed as far as paint supplies, in order to get an idea of where we would put everything.

When we pulled into the driveway, I was in absolute shock. I didn't remember the house being so small. It was 960 square feet. We got inside the house and I was an absolute mess; I walked through the house by myself. When I got to the back room, the door to that room had a window onto the backyard. I just stared out the window. I had so much going on in my head. My initial thought was what in the world have we done! I don't know how long I stood there, but the real estate agent walked up behind me, put her arm around my shoulder, and just kept saying, "Gabe it will be alright, everything will work out." That helped a little bit, because I was ready to jump back in the truck and head south again.

I managed to compose myself enough to join everyone else, and we continued looking around the house. Finished looking, we headed back to the hotel. We sat and talked for a while. My sister was driving home on Sunday afternoon. Our initial plan was for my mom and me to head back to Florida on Sunday. But there was no way I could go back Sunday. My mom had to get back to work Monday so she rented a car and drove back Sunday morning.

We closed on the house that Monday afternoon. After closing, we went over to the house and made a list of what we needed for paint and supplies. We worked on the house that week while we stayed in the hotel and moved in shortly thereafter. That following Sunday, I headed back to Florida to work out my final weeks' notice. I did not want to leave Connie there by herself, but I had no choice.

As soon as my last week at work had ended, I headed back to Asheville. We concentrated our efforts in organizing the house and settling in. It was now time for us to start the job-hunting expedition.

CHAPTER 6

Two-Cheeseburger Value Meal

CONNIE AND I WOULD go to a fast-food restaurant and order a two-cheeseburger value meal, which was a treat for us. We would place the order, pay with change we saved up, find a shady spot in the parking lot, and sit and enjoy our feast. The time we spent sitting there talking to each other was priceless; it drew us closer than ever. I hold those times close to my heart. (For more about this time, see Chapter 13, "Asheville Adjustment," in Connie's book.) Even though our fast-food meal cost very little, it was like date night with us. We were excited and happy to go out.

How about you? When is the last time you went out? When was the last time you did something simple: no restaurant, just sitting, not hurried, and talking to your spouse—enjoying each other's company? I am talking about engaging with your spouse and being present with them, not on your cell phone. You watch them eat their fries and share your soda (no backwash either). If you will take the time out of your busy schedule to do this or something similar, you will build memories that will last a lifetime. Trust me, in the long run it will pay off; sometimes you have to keep it simple.

I know now, years later, what phenomenal times they were. We would remind ourselves of things we learned and declare we would not forget where we came from and what we went through.

It amazes me how God in His infinite wisdom prepared us in Florida. We purchased good things and saw how He made them last. We would have been in a world of hurt otherwise, as there was no extra money to buy anything.

Never in a million years did we think it would take a while for us to find jobs. Connie didn't want to go back into nursing unless she had to. I had worked in the automotive field for many years. I tried everywhere to find a job; it seemed like I submitted a thousand or so applications. The only place that called me was a home improvement store, so I accepted the position. At that time, Connie wanted to have a bed-and-breakfast, so she found a position as a concierge. The pay was not that great, but she was looking for the experience so we could open one later. Staying in a bed-and-breakfast is charming, but behind the scenes of ownership is a whole other thing. You are committed seven days a week to be successful. Connie discovered she didn't want to do this after all.

We knew it was only a matter of time before she would have to go back to nursing. I kept looking for a higher paying job but was not successful. We could not make ends meet.

Connie started putting in applications at doctors' offices. That did not work out well. Her work experience and years as a nurse made her overqualified for a position. Many places would not even talk to her because they thought she would require a higher pay scale than they wanted to offer. She did have a few interviews, but nothing worked out. Here was a nurse looking for a job and no one wanted to hire her. Nurses were in demand, so the news said. Go figure.

I had a day off and persuaded Connie to try the hospital for employment. I knew the town better, so I went with her. She had her mind made up that she wanted to work days and no nights. Twenty years of working nights in intensive care was enough for her, plus the one doctor in Florida said she needed to get away from working nights. He was very serious about it.

We arrived at the hospital and were directed to human resources. I sat in the waiting room. A while later, someone came out of the office with Connie. As they walked, Connie looked at me and I could tell she was not a happy camper. Oh boy! I wondered what was going on. She came back a while later and we left the hospital. On the drive home, she went into detail. She had a job, which was somewhat of a relief.

I had always known that Connie would make more money than me and I was okay with that. I was not insecure about it; it was a fact. I had issues with Connie having to go back to the hospital in the first place, knowing she did not want to. The doctors also wanted her to get out of the stress of nursing. With my job, I could not provide enough to support us financially. I did everything I could; this was just the way it was working out. I was going to have to deal with that. It is hard for men when they can't provide for their family. It is the way we are designed, to be providers. I could not keep her out of nursing.

It was awhile before I felt better about it. I had to once again trust God that He would take care of her and protect her. One book I read, *The Silence of Adam,* by Dr. Larry Crabb, helped me understand myself and become a better man. I have given this excellent book to many men over the years. It helps you to trust God in the dark times in your life.

There are always times in life where you are forced to grow, like it or not. It always comes down to how you choose to deal with these times. For me, in this situation, I could deal with it or push it aside. If you choose the latter and don't deal with it, it will arrive again in your life and you will have the same choice every time. The situations will sometimes get harder and tougher. I have learned, with Connie's help, to hit things head on and deal with the issue at hand. Once you do, you feel better and can move on, not having it in the back of your mind. I did work through it.

It was a while before we got back on our feet and had more than forty dollars per month for groceries. After that, when we went back to the drive-thru, both of us were able to get our very own meals. We had committed to each other to never forget this time in our lives by being aware of people around us who were going through the same thing we did, and remember to help them and pray for them.

Over the next year or so, we were able to do some little projects around the house like painting, yard work, and gardening. We loved to do things like this together. We worked very well together and had a lot of fun.

One project we did was building a small deck off the back porch. On the end of the porch was a six-foot by five-foot concrete pad on the ground. We built the deck and attached it to the porch. Little did we know how much it would get used! We also did not know that everything we had gone through over the last few years was all in preparation for what lay ahead.

CHAPTER 7

You Have Got to Be Kidding Me!

AT HER HOSPITAL JOB, Connie had been able to get a daylight shift working four days, twelve hours each shift. She was on a very busy floor. After having worked a couple of years on that floor, one day she started telling me her right shoulder was stiff and sore.

The next day at work, Connie ran into one of her doctors on the floor and mentioned the pain in her shoulder to him. He wanted to see her in his office. When she got home, she told me about running into the doctor and what he said. We talked about it and didn't feel too worried. It took a little while for her to get the appointment.

The day of the appointment arrived and the doctor did the normal things like blood work and all the preliminary stuff they routinely do. Then he examined under her right arm and felt that the lymph nodes were different, so he ordered X-rays. When we received the results that they didn't appear to be normal, the next step was a biopsy. Dr. Michaels recommended Dr. Donaldson for the biopsy as well as possible plastic surgery. Additionally, he recommended Dr. Roberts, the oncology surgeon to remove the cancer if it came to that.

We were a bit shaken but were optimistic about the outcome. I kept telling myself it was just a routine biopsy and everything would be okay. Connie made an appointment with Dr. Donaldson to get the biopsy done.

Two weeks later, the day of the biopsy arrived and we went to the outpatient center to do all the normal things like registering. We prayed before Connie when into surgery. We both felt good about it. The biopsy took only about an hour. The doctor came out and told us we would now have to wait for the lab results.

The days in between the biopsy and going back to see Dr. Donaldson were rather interesting, to say the least. We went through a range of emotions. We would stand strong in our faith but sometimes think about the possibility of it being cancer. Finally, we had our appointment and were taken to one of the exam rooms to wait for Dr. Donaldson. After a bit of small talk, he told Connie it was cancer. Wow! Talk about taking the wind out of your sails. No matter how many times I have heard it said, it is still the worst possible word you can have in your ears. The rest of the conversation was somewhat of a blur, as I was in shock. He mentioned something about a surgeon to remove the cancer and he would do the breast reconstruction. The whole surgery would take three to four hours.

It was a quiet ride home as we both tried to compose our thoughts and wrap our heads around all of this. Little did I know how much our lives would change by one word: cancer! Cancer doesn't take into account: age, income, race or gender. It changes everyone's life in one way or another. It was a day or two before we talked about it extensively. Connie was very good about relating to me what the medical terms meant and what was going to happen. I thought I had a handle on it. I didn't know that my role as a man and husband would forever change. A note to all men out there dealing with this: A lot will change for you with this kind of situation and you have to dig deep within you to carry on.

I had been a Christian all my life and I totally believed Connie would be healed. I had to believe that still and stand upon it. I had to support her any way I could. I knew God would help me with that. There is no book or manual on how to support and take care of your spouse. It was only God and me. If you think I was rock solid all the time, let me tell you, I had to fight against the head games that began in my mind. It is those little thoughts that creep in that you have to battle in order to stay strong.

One thing I loved about Connie was that once she dealt with things, she would ask me how I was doing. I knew I had better have good answers; otherwise, she would not let it go until she saw I was okay with everything. I understood I had time to get myself in order before we would talk about it. I learned not to give her pat answers because she would only dig deeper. She kept me on my toes. The quicker you deal with the issues the quicker you can move on; otherwise, the communication between you and your wife breaks down. Marriage is all about communicating. When going through something like this, you need the lines of communication open at all times. Men, if you don't talk to her about the issues, you are only cheating, robbing, and short-changing yourself of intimacy in your marriage.

I thought I knew how strong Connie was by the way she dealt with issues and moved on. I saw how incredibly strong she was.

It was going to be a month before the operation could be done. I felt like that was a good thing because it gave us time to get more of a handle on this cancer issue. Connie went back to work, which was good, as it kept her busy. For me, it helped me not get wound up and helped me keep things in perspective.

CHAPTER 8

Alone

We discussed whether Connie wanted family to be there for the surgery as support for her. After thinking about it for some time, she decided she didn't want anyone there besides me because she didn't think it would be a big deal.

The day of the surgery arrived all too soon. When you are in a situation like this, you think in the back of your mind that you don't want this day to be here; but here it is, whether you like it or not, and off you go. All the pre-op went without a hitch. In the holding cell, as I like to call it, nurses came in and out, asking a thousand and one necessary probing questions while putting in the IVs. We prayed and tried to keep the atmosphere light.

When they came to take her for surgery, an array of emotions from fear to anxiety went through my mind. All the while, I was trying to keep my emotions together. I kissed her and told her I would see her later. I then headed to the waiting room with a bag of Connie's clothes and a book I had brought along to read—like I could concentrate on reading! Oh well, it kept me busy for a while anyway. I settled in for the wait. The majority of the time I spent waiting for the volunteer to call for me saying the surgery went well, she is in recovery, and should be in her room in a little while. Besides that, I spent time praying, attempting to read, and looking around the waiting room at the rest of the people. I knew they were going through the same thing or at least something similar.

This was not to be one of those days where there was going to be a short wait.

In an hour or so, Dr. Roberts came down and escorted me to one of the little rooms. He said his part of the surgery went well. They were able to remove all the cancer. He stated the reconstruction should be about another hour and a half. I had a huge sigh of relief followed with a "Thank you, Jesus." On the way back to the waiting room, a little of my anxiety went away.

The waiting room in the hospital was located by an exit the doctors and nurses used. About an hour and a half went by and I saw Dr. Donaldson's nurse exiting the hospital. I thought that was odd since I had not received a call. Okay, relax, I told myself; the phone will ring for you. Another half hour went by. Finally, there was a call for me: "Connie is in the recovery room. We will call you shortly." I was relieved for only a little while, as I received another call saying Connie was having a hard time waking up.

Our family home group leader from the Rock of Asheville Church we attended stopped by to check on me. The volunteer called me to the phone once more. This time the message was that I needed to go to the recovery room. I asked for directions and he accompanied me.

We arrived at a set of swinging doors with a sign above them: Recovery Room. A male nurse came out asking for me. He told me the doctor would like to speak to me. He went back in and a few seconds later a doctor I wasn't familiar with came out. To this day, I still don't remember his name. In his left hand, he held an X-ray up to the light. He told me it was an X-ray of Connie's lungs. He informed me that her right lung had collapsed. If he didn't put in a chest tube immediately, she would die. He was short, sweet, and to the point. I will never forget that. I absolutely froze. I felt shock, terror, and anxiety all wrapped up in one. All I could manage to say was "Fix her." He left as fast as he came.

Alone, standing there, I looked over at our family group leader. There was a look of horror on his face. No words were spoken because he was as stunned as I. The nurse came back with a consent form and told me I needed to sign it so the doctor could put the chest tube in. I immediately signed it and handed it back to him. He asked if I would like to see Connie. I think he saw what had taken place and felt sorry for me. As I followed the nurse through the double doors, I felt numb; I couldn't even think.

There were about six beds on my right and left. I immediately saw Dr. Donaldson and Dr. Smith standing by the last bed on the right. It all seemed like a bad dream. That walk to her bed seemed to take forever. At Connie's bedside, the doctors were working away feverishly.

I felt completely helpless and not in control of anything. Everything had happened so quickly that I couldn't even think. Dr. Donaldson spoke to me and told me it would be alright. Other than that, I have no idea what he said. It just didn't register. Connie was in the twilight zone, but she recognized my voice; she raised her left hand up to touch me. Our hands touched momentarily before her hand went limp as she dozed back off.

I left the room and walked back into the hallway, not knowing how I got there. I noticed our home group leader hadn't left. We walked through the waiting room to go outside. I tried to explain to him the best I could, what I could remember. He prayed with me before leaving. Inside of me, I didn't want him to leave, but I knew he had to go. I was alone. I tried to call my mom, but she was at work. I made several more calls trying to reach someone, but everyone was at work. I tried to pray, but the only words I could get out were: "God, what's going on? Help! Please help me."

Alone, all alone. People were around, but no one was there for me. I finally realized it was just God and me. My innermost being was shaken to the very core. My God whom I trust was letting this happen. Why?

He was silent. I knew He was there with me, but I could not feel Him. I wanted Him to hold me, but that wouldn't happen. Alone.

I stayed outside for a while, trying to compose myself. I knew I had to go back into the waiting room. I finally reached the point where I could go back inside. I tried to organize myself the best I could, but my mind was going a thousand miles an hour. Thoughts were bombarding my mind like "If Connie dies, what I will do?" My mind was now a battlefield; the war was in full rage. I was trying to cling to what I knew: God. I was clinging to what I had learned over my lifetime with Him. But then the thoughts poured in again that Connie was going to die. I would retaliate in my mind and say NO, but back and forth the thoughts went relentlessly. Fear was now trying to set in. I was trying so hard not to lose control of my emotions. Some time went by. I received another call from the recovery room nurse. She said Connie was doing well. She told me the room number where they would bring Connie in a few minutes. I hung up the phone and dashed to the elevator. I arrived in Connie's room before she got there. Dr. Donaldson came in the room and asked if I was okay. He also wanted to know what the other doctor had said. After I told him, he said it was not that serious. He emphasized that what I had been told was true, but things were now under control. I was in the room by myself for a little while. Thank God for that. My world was turned upside down. How was I to know it was not that serious? I still felt helpless and not in control of anything. No one was there to comfort me; I was alone. Nothing made any sense. I realized how fragile life is. I thought about what was important in my life. I first thought about my relationship with Jesus Christ and then I thought about my wife, family, and friends. Everything else was not important; it all seemed meaningless. If I lost everything else, it would not change anything. All the possessions I had could be acquired again. There is a verse in the Bible that sums it up: "Meaningless! Meaningless!" says the Teacher. Everything is meaningless!" (Ecclesiastes 12:8; New International Version [NIV]).

I truly understood what He was saying. We think we can't live without all the possessions, but we can. Connie could not be replaced if I lost her; therefore, I would have lost everything in life. Wow, I had some time to think on that.

Noises startled me and interrupted my thoughts. An entourage of nurses brought Connie into the room. I was not prepared for what I saw. There were lots of hoses, lines, and chords everywhere. I don't remember how long it took to get her situated, but it seemed like forever. I wanted desperately to be close to her and spend time with her. I could have lost her. When everyone finally left the room, I walked over to her bed, leaned over, and kissed her on the forehead. I looked at her and felt my helplessness again. There was nothing I could do, so I began to pray. I was defenseless and vulnerable feeling so helpless, knowing there is nothing in this world you can do for the one you love. I could do nothing, but trusted that God was there and He would take care of her. Even though I knew that, it was so hard for me to let go; I wanted to help Him. I wanted Him to fix her right then so we could go home.

I reluctantly left the hospital for a little while to go home and let the dog out and feed her. Our dog was named Jasmine, but we called her Jaz. She was a hundred-pound Rottweiler. I inherited her when we married. You hear so much negative about Rottweilers, but she was the best dog I ever had. Jasmine was well trained and loved Connie. I never worried about Connie being alone because Jasmine protected her.

I made my way back to the hospital.

CHAPTER 9

Hospital 101

PRIOR TO THIS INSTANCE, I had been in hospitals with Connie a couple of times. I was with her for the first lumpectomy and then for a cyst on her ovaries. When she had the cyst removed, she had to stay overnight in the hospital. She worked at Delray Beach Hospital. She did not want a lot of people in the hospital to know what was going on with her so she had her doctor move her somewhere else in the hospital instead of the general surgery floor. Can you guess where he put her? The maternity ward! Yes, he did, in the maternity ward, of all places. For someone who never wanted children to be placed in the maternity ward was hilarious. We laughed about that for years.

Now back to our story: The journey back to our house to tend to Jasmine was a blur. I was able to contact family and let everyone know what was happening, though. Walking back into the hospital room and seeing Connie connected to what looked like a thousand and one hoses and tubes, not to mention IV pumps, was once again shocking. She was sleeping and I just stood staring at her.

Connie slept most of the time I was there. She would wake up, look around to see me, and doze off again. There was no conversation between us, so I had a significant portion of time to think and pray. Too much thinking can be detrimental. Many of the thoughts I battled involved being scared, helpless, and, of course, facing the unknown. I was emotionally drained.

Sometimes all I could do was gaze at Connie and pray. I was both numb and distressed. I could not think very well, so it was a good thing I did not have to make any decisions at that time. I also knew that I could not stay the night with her because I had to take care of the pets. In addition to Jasmine, we had a cat named Chan. I did not want to leave Connie! It tore my heart out to have to be in two places at one time.

The following day, Connie was a little more coherent. She was on a morphine pump that she controlled. Just one push of the button and it was good night for her. She was in a lot of pain due to the chest tube, but we were able to talk a little bit amidst her naps.

She was in Mission St. Joseph Hospital, where she worked, so a lot of her coworkers were able to visit her. Let me impart knowledge concerning something I learned from this experience: When going to visit someone in the hospital, be very mindful of what they are going through by paying attention to the length of time you are there. They need rest in order to get better. Long visits tire them. In our case, the second day after surgery, Connie was not in good enough shape to have visitors. The people she worked with only stayed a few minutes, as they understood this principle. Others stayed for quite some time, waiting for her to wake up in order to try and talk to her. She just did not have the stamina yet to visit with people.

After a while I, with God's help, figured this out. I would monitor the situation if needed and would ask people very nicely to leave and possibly come back later due to her stamina. Some of you might think this is rude, but it is not. Connie did not have the energy to hold conversations; they were very draining for her. It took everything she had just to eat some food.

One day you might encounter a situation when you are in that bed and you may be very thankful I wrote about this.

We were so grateful to everyone who came to see Connie. Some of our friends drove over a half hour and only stayed ten minutes. Everyone was understanding about making their visits short.

Over the next few days, some of the tubes and IVs were removed. I remember the day the chest tube was removed. Connie did not want me in the room, as she knew it wouldn't be good for me to see that. The head nurse entered and asked Connie's permission for some nursing students to watch the tube being removed. Chest tubes are not too common, so Connie agreed, as long as the tube came out.

I left the room and waited in the hall. I watched the instructor with a group of nursing students enter the room. They were in there about ten minutes and then left. I thought that was quick. When I entered the room, Connie said that the tube hurt when it came out. She said, "I know that I have pulled a few chest tubes in my days as a nurse and the patients always said it hurt. They were not kidding! It is different when you are the patient; I now understand."

Connie was in the hospital about a week. She was more than ready after that to go home. The people at the hospital were diligent in their care of Connie. I am ever so thankful of how well they took care of her.

When she was released, Connie went home with a drain coming out of her right side. It was there to remove any fluid that would collect after the surgery. It was a small tube attached to a ball. She would empty the ball, squeeze it, and then reattach it so there'd be suction to draw the fluid out. The other part of the surgery involved putting a "port" in the upper section of her left shoulder. It was placed under the skin and attached to the muscle. It was square in shape and attached to a major artery. This was an access point for the nurses to draw blood and to administer chemotherapy so they did not have to start IVs every time Connie had a treatment. These two things were not comfortable, especially when Connie tried to sleep.

She could not find a comfortable position, so she wasn't able to sleep well. It was not until they removed the drain that she slept better.

It was fantastic to have Connie home. I know the cat and the dog were glad, as they clung to her like glue for the first few days. Mom is home!

This surgery was very rough on Connie. She was very tired with not much energy. A good day for her was to make coffee and walk to the computer room where all her books were. Connie was an avid reader. Her big bookcase contained a massive amount of books: mysteries, Shakespeare, Christian, gardening and home Improvement, poetry, self-help, music, art, and more. Her other favorite spot where she spent a lot of time was the small deck we had built to one side of the back porch. We had placed privacy lattice around two sides. Connie had her plants in deck boxes that hung off the railing. The deck was a safe haven for her.

As for me, I was charting unknown waters as a caretaker. My life and the way I saw everything was about to change. Connie and I did almost everything together, from cooking (our kitchen was really small, so it took us a while to get used to working so closely in a confined space; I called it the kitchen dance) and shopping to housework and yard work. It was time spent together. We worked well as a team and really loved it. I would now have to do almost everything, which I did not mind at all since she couldn't. I would, however, miss doing those things together. Yes, Connie was there, but it was not the same. I would spend a lot of time thanking God for Connie and for bringing her home, however. I was not alone.

On a Sunday morning about six weeks after the operation, Connie noticed her left arm swelling, which puzzled her. She thought complications, if any, would occur on the side where the surgery had taken place, not the opposite side. It wasn't severely swollen, so she ignored the situation and went to bed that evening thinking it was nothing. The next morning, she awoke to find her left arm extremely swollen. She called me at work, told me about it, and said she was probably going to get X-rays taken. She didn't think it was a big deal, so I felt okay about not going with her.

When she contacted her oncology surgeon, he expressed concern that there was a blockage in the venous access device. She went in right away to the radiology department at the hospital and proceeded to have a dye test and X-rays taken. Five blood clots were discovered, primarily within the blood vessels of the chest, one in the vessel going into the neck, and one around the venous access device itself. The doctor immediately began treating her with a blood thinner in the form of an injection. I knew nothing about this until I got home from work and she filled me in. She had not been able to take the time to call me, as time had been of the essence. I was shocked. This was a very serious situation and it made both of us nervous. We knew full well what could potentially happen if these blood clots broke loose. Recovery was dangerous and there was a small chance it could be fatal. Connie gave herself injections twice a day for a week followed by regular doses of oral blood thinner.

Now she was on the road to recovery again and life was returning to a type of normalcy.

CHAPTER 10

Chemo, Round One

AT ONE OF CONNIE'S follow-up doctors' appointments, Dr. Michaels showed us where her chemo would be administered. He led us to the back of the building to a very large room. The nurse's station was on the left along a back wall while the rest of the room was open. A semicircle of a dozen or so big recliners faced the back wall. The back wall was three-quarter glass from top to bottom, revealing a fountain with flowing water that started on the outside then stopped at the glass. Another part of the fountain started on the inside of the glass. When you were in the room, it looked like the two fountains were actually one. In the center of the room was a black baby grand piano with an acoustic guitar beside it. Students from the local college would play for the patients. We took notice of the patients in the recliners and people sitting with them. It was a very comfortable room.

Thursday was the day of the chemo appointment and it was already here. We were both really nervous. Connie and I talked a lot about this, but I still wonder what really went through her mind. I may never know.

We were introduced to Joanna who was to be Connie's nurse for her chemo treatments. Joanna was a middle-aged woman who had been a nurse for a long time. She, too, had lived in south Florida and then moved to Asheville. The more Connie and Joanna talked the more similarities they discovered. It was like they had known each other for years. That connection would help Connie a lot.

Joanna escorted us to one of the recliners on the right side of the semicircle. Next to the recliners were chairs for others to sit. Joanna went over all the pros and cons of the chemo, how it was administered, the reactions, how most people feel, and how to deal with the most common side effects. If there would be any side effects, they would start about three days after the treatment. Four rounds of chemo would be administered to Connie.

When Joanna was finished talking with us, she hooked Connie up to the first of many bags of fluids delivered through the port that had been inserted during the surgery. I was really nervous and prayed the whole time. It would take a few hours for the chemo to be completed. Connie was somewhat quiet for the first part and so was I. Another chapter in our life was starting.

I sat there and wondered if the chemo would work. I wondered whether we had done enough to prepare for this. I wondered if Connie would have any of those side effects mentioned. There was a women sitting to our left who was getting chemo. Every so often she would vomit into a small trash can. I was praying for her and also began praying that Connie would not get sick like that. In the chapter "First Treatment" in Connie's book, *The Courage to Be Imperfect,* she elaborates on what she went through at this treatment.

It seemed like it took forever for the chemo to be completed. I looked at my watch and then looked at the pump pushing the drugs. Man, was it slow. Why couldn't they speed that pump up? I wanted it to be finished already so we could get out of there. Beep beep, beep beep came a continual sound when the pump finished a bag. Joanna would remove the bag and hook another bag up to the pump. I kept wondering how many bags there were to go through. I tried to relax and keep my mind busy. There were headsets for the patients to listen to music or magazines to read if they chose. Drinks and crackers were also provided.

Finally, the last bag was finished and we could go home. Connie was depleted and exhausted. They gave her some drugs to take home with her to help with any side effects that arose. Friday and Saturday for Connie was not too bad, though she was tired and didn't have much energy. At that point, we thought she might not get the side effects and we were praying she would not.

Sunday morning, Connie ran for the bathroom. She had taken all the drugs they gave her to combat nausea, but they did not work. The next few days were very challenging, to say the least. Connie got sick at the least little smell. Her sense of smell was heightened. She did not eat a lot and she had a hard time keeping down fluids. She needed those fluids desperately. This lasted for a couple of days, which left her very weak and tired. It all seemed unreal to me. She could keep nothing in her stomach.

First the mastectomy, then the blood clots, now this? I asked the Lord, "How much more can she take?" I felt so helpless! Once again, it was a trust issue with God and me. I knew He would take care of her. All I could do was to be there for her and listen for His still small voice that would lead me to do what needed to be done. He already knew what she needed.

After a few days, the sickness started to subside. She was so tired and weak from the loss of fluids and not eating much, however, that she slept for long periods of time. When she would get up, she did not have much energy to walk far, so she would either sit on the back deck if the weather was nice, in the study at the computer, or on a chair and read.

It was hard to cook anything that would not make her nauseous. In order for her to eat at all and not smell the aroma of the food, she had to eat outside or have the ceiling fan on to keep the smells away. I had to cook for myself, which was no big deal, but I had to cook with the kitchen door open or make something that did not take long to cook. After a couple of weeks, she started to feel like herself. Eating was still an issue, though, as she wasn't hungry. She literally had to make herself eat and drink fluids.

Watching Connie go through this was heart-wrenching. I wanted to wave my magic wand and make it all go away, but my magic wand did not work. It is unbelievably hard and frustrating to be the caretaker in a situation like this. My hands were tied as to what I could do for her. There were times I wanted to pick her up and carry her away someplace, so she would not have to go through that, but the reality was I could not. I did not mind the extra things I had to do around the house as long as she got better. I got tired of asking Connie how she was feeling. I knew she felt the same way. I just wanted to keep up with how she was feeling so I could figure out a way to help her. I think these times deepened my trust and faith in God by knowing He knew where we were at and what we were going through. Sometimes all I could do was just breathe.

A couple of weeks before the next treatment, Connie and I decided to go on the Hallelujah Diet by George Malkmus. It was a vegetarian diet, which was certainly a change for us. You were to eat a lot of raw fruits and vegetables. We ate a salad almost every day plus other dishes we would make. One part of this diet was juicing. Connie started drinking an eight-ounce glass of carrot juice every morning with half an apple added to it for flavor. She would drink three-quarters of it and then add one tablespoon of Barley Green. One tip I will share concerning the carrots is to peel the skin off the carrots with a potato peeler, so your hands won't turn orange from the carrots. A cancer patient can't have pulp anyway, so that is another reason for peeling the carrots.

The second treatment arrived just a few days before Christmas. Connie always scheduled her appointments as late in the day as she could so I could go with her. We arrived for our appointment and they got Connie hooked up and settled in. It was very nice to watch the staff finishing up the Christmas decorations. Some of the doctors and the physician's assistant even helped decorate. Connie was the last person still getting her chemo. It was about 5:30 or 6:00 p.m. Dr. Michaels came into the room, saw we were still there, got a stool, and sat and talked to us until the chemo was complete. We talked about a lot of things, especially photography. We all loved to shoot photography. This was such a cool thing, as most of the time during our appointments, he was too busy to chat like that.

At another treatment, a young man from the college played the piano for the patients. He was majoring in music and was very talented. Again we were the last ones there for this appointment. He played the piano for a while and then quit, picked up his guitar, grabbed a stool, and came over to where we sitting. He asked Connie if she had something in particular she'd like to hear and he'd play that for her.

Following that, Dr. Michaels appeared out of nowhere and joined our conversation. We discovered that he, too, played guitar. That is all Connie needed to hear—the game was on! She talked him into playing for her, so he sat down and played for a while. The remaining staff was shocked. They gathered around to listen. None of them knew that he played the guitar. That was such a memorable experience and one of the bright spots during her chemo.

Well, Merry Christmas to us on Christmas Day. Connie's symptoms started: nausea and then fatigue, but there were no trips to the bathroom. The only thing we had changed was our diet and Connie drinking carrot juice with Barley Green. We could not believe how much difference there was. We knew we were onto something. This was encouraging. The week after Christmas, however, Connie noticed that her hair started to fall out. She noticed it on her pillow when she woke up and noticed even more when she brushed her hair. Her hair continued to fall out, leading up to the Bad Hair Day.

CHAPTER 11

Bad Hair Day

HAIR LOSS WAS ONE of the side effects that Joanna the nurse had covered during our first chemotherapy treatment. It was the major side effect on this round. Let me tell you, Connie did not handle that news well. You have to go back to her high school days to understand the significance of this. She received an award for the most beautiful hair in her class. She had long blonde hair down to the middle of her back. I knew her hair was very important to her. It was always so beautiful.

Joanna told Connie that some people had success with various kinds of shampoos. She suggested that Connie cut her hair shorter so there would be less weight. The search was on to find the shampoo. We acquired it from her salon. The next step was considering cutting her hair. A lot of time was spent looking at hairstyles in magazines, books, and the internet. We even bought a computer program that allowed you to place a photo of yourself so you could "try on" different hairdos. We did have a lot of fun with that.

Connie finally arrived at a decision on the final hairdo. She made the hair appointment to have it cut short. She was determined not to lose her hair. She did look good in short hair. I think it took both of us awhile to get used to it, since it was a change. She faithfully used the shampoo and did what she could.

Even though her hair started to fall out gradually, she would not give up. She was careful how she brushed it, but it continued falling out. I knew she was really struggling. Her hair was such a part of who she was. Once in conversation she talked about shaving it all off, but I knew that would not happen. As the treatments progressed, she experienced more and more hair loss. She was not handling it well.

One night Connie went to take her shower. I heard her muttering in there about something. "GABE!" was the next thing I heard. I raced into the bathroom. Connie pulled the shower curtain back a little bit and had me look at what was happening. Connie ran her hand through her wet hair and a huge fist full of hair came out in her hand. I will never forget the look on her face. My heart sank and, helpless, I did not know what to say.

She looked at me and said, "I can't handle this. You have to cut my hair off. Please!"

I was not sure how my face looked, but I froze for a moment. I couldn't believe what I was hearing.

She said it again. "Cut my hair off. I can't handle seeing it go down the drain and seeing myself in the mirror like this."

All I could say was okay. I spun around and left the bathroom. I told myself I couldn't do this, that I wouldn't be able to hold it together enough to do this. I told myself to suck it up, that I did not have a choice here; I had to do this.

It was around 8:00 p.m. I had to think quickly what we needed and what we had. I found two pairs of old scissors, a wooden chair, and my little black electric mustache trimmer. I placed the chair in the kitchen, and waited for Connie. Thank God, I had a little time before she finished her shower to collect myself, as I was a wreck. I felt numb. I told God that He'd have to give me the strength to do this.

When Connie walked into the kitchen, her hair was a mess. There were bald spots here and there. She sat down and I wrapped a towel around her shoulders. She held it closed with her hand. I asked her if she was sure she wanted me to do this.

"If you do not want to, I will do it myself," she replied.

I told her I'd do it. I knew she was on the verge of losing it.

When we arrived in Asheville (before all of this happened), she had a difficult time finding someone to cut her hair the way she liked it. She tried several different beauticians. I said in jest that she could let me cut it. We laughed about that. I never dreamt I would be standing behind her with scissors in my hand.

I proceeded to cut away. The first pair of scissors was dull and would not cut two cents' worth. I tried a second pair, but they weren't any better. Oh boy! I kept using them both until I figured out I was going to have to cut a little at a time. We had become quiet, despite the fact that I was cutting away, knowing if one of us said the wrong thing, we'd both lose it. I was sick to my stomach thinking about cutting off her beautiful hair! If someone had told me a few years before that I would be doing this, I would have considered that absurd.

As I was praying for the Lord to help me through this, I asked Him why I had to be the one to do this. I told Him this was not fun and I wanted this merry-go-round to stop and let us off. I was finally making some progress with those dull scissors. I could feel the tears welling up inside me. This was immensely difficult. I had to tell myself to get a grip, focus, and not think about what I was doing. Focus, Gabe, and keep cutting.

What do you talk about when you are in this situation? I didn't know what to say. I said, "Lord, I need you to give me something to say to lighten up this situation as this is getting way too hard." Finally, after a moment, I said, "You told me I would never cut your hair, but look at what I'm doing now. Well, you asked me." She was silent for a moment, then chuckled and said, "Yes, I did." That seemed to break the silence of the situation. I can't even imagine what was going through Connie's mind. We were able to chat a little bit.

The Lord is good and does help us in a time of need. Once we started talking, everything started to change. We kept the conversation light. We actually began having some fun with it. It is a good thing I did not get paid for this because it was a really bad haircut, totally uneven. Oh well, I continued cutting. We were also having to battle with the cat and dog to keep them out of the kitchen. They were tromping through the hair and tracking it all over the house. They wanted to be with us and in on what was going on.

It is astonishing how animals know when things get rough. I've seen it time and time again. Anytime Connie would not feel good, they were both right there, wanting to be with her. The dog would come over and put her head in Connie's lap and look up at her.

I finally had Connie's hair as close as I could get it with the scissors. I then took the black mustache trimmer and began buzz-cutting the quarter inch or so of hair that was left. This was interesting, to say the least, as the trimmer was not made for that. With a little time, I got most of the hair and then used my electric razor to shave off the stubble. That took some time. Finally, all Connie's hair was off. She got up and walked straight to the bathroom. She was quiet.

I did not follow her because I knew she needed some time to get used to it. I started cleaning up. After a little while, she came back out and said that was better and she could deal with it. It was like someone flipped a switch in her. She was almost back to normal. I just stared at her for a second, seeing her bald for the first time face-to-face. It was the way she smiled at me that put me at ease. I do not know what happened in the bathroom, but that is the way she was. She was able to move on and accept it. For me, that was one of the most difficult things I'd had to do at that point in my life. When you are forced into difficult situations, it is surprising what you can do.

We were both wiped out emotionally and physically. We definitely did not anticipate what was going to happen that day. Connie said she wanted to go to the mall the next day to find some bandanas to wear. Morning came soon enough. We went to the mall and looked around. We did buy a few. Connie started to get tired. We knew she had only so much energy, so we had to plan our day wisely. In the last store, I looked around and saw a display of her favorite chocolates. Connie wandered into another section so I snuck off and bought a box of truffles. I told the clerk I was going to put them in my jacket instead of a bag as my wife was in the store with me and I wanted to surprise her with them. We left the store, got in the car, and I handed Connie the box of truffles. I told her after what she just went through, I thought she'd really needed them. She was quiet for a moment and then ripped into the box, saying, "Yes, I do." We sat in the parking lot for a while eating a few truffles and talking about the events that had taken place.

Connie found a wig online and bought it sight unseen for around twenty dollars. She said she was not going to pay a lot of money for something she would not wear all the time. My sister Rose came down for a visit not long after this bad hair day and cut Connie's wig so it looked better on her. Rose had been a beautician for years. The wig did look pretty good. Rose commented that Connie was the most beautiful bald woman she had ever seen. This comment made an impact on Connie because she knew Rose would not say it if she didn't mean it.

I offered to get my head shaved to support Connie. I was serious about doing that. Connie would not hear of it. She told me she knew I supported her and I didn't need to do that. She told me she liked my hair and didn't want me bald. I never did have it shaved off.

CHAPTER 12

Thursday Mornings

As I THINK BACK about what helped me through all these rough times, it was the time I spent with God. I tried to spend time with Him in reading the Bible, praying, and also in praise and worship, which helped me most of all. Sometimes I did not know what to pray or what to say to God. "You have searched me, Lord, and you know me. You know when I sit and when I rise; you perceive my thoughts from afar." (Psalm 139:1–2; New International Version [NIV]). He knew how I was feeling, what was going on inside me, and all the questions I had.

Praise and worship is focusing on who He is and how great He is. It is not asking for anything; it is enjoying His presence. You can sing to Him or just thank Him for all He has done for you. It is like crawling up in His lap and He holds you. It is you knowing He is there and He knows where you're at.

The church we were attending in Asheville was a contemporary, nondenominational church. As a drummer, I wanted to get involved in the music department. Playing drums was one of my passions. They did not really need a drummer because the youth pastor was the main drummer and he had a backup. They wanted to fit me in somehow so they asked me if I wanted to play for the Thursday morning prayer group. They had a hard time finding someone who could be there at 6:00 a.m. I said I would because I started work at 7:00 a.m. and the church was just a few miles from work. I accepted their offer and when I went into work, I asked my boss if it was okay if I came in Thursdays at 7:15 a.m.; she said it would not be a problem. This way I could have a little time playing before my workday began. I was excited to play again.

My first Thursday morning, I did not know what to expect. I found out we would have singing first and then, after a few songs, people would pray out loud for different needs that had been mentioned at the start of the service. I was given a list of songs we were going to sing. I found out soon enough not to rely on the list because the person leading worship would change the songs on the fly. I liked that a lot; it was very spontaneous so I never knew what to expect. Some of the songs we sang on Sundays, so I had no chance to rehearse. The worship leader would just start the song and away we went; it was fun.

I finally found where I belonged in the church. I was not playing to the large crowds on Sunday mornings. On Thursdays, if we had twenty people, that was huge. At times, it would be the keyboard player and me or a guitar player and me. They found a bass player who could also attend. We were all excited about that, as he fit right in with us.

I had started this Thursday morning drumming before Connie had any health issues. When the health problems started and the prayer group found out about them, they supported me in many ways. They prayed for Connie all the time. Usually, the person leading would ask for an update before the service started. They would pray for both of us, which meant the world to me.

For me, this was an hour once a week when I did not have any problems; I would try to release them to God and let Him deal with them all for a while. In the Bible, it says, "Come to me all you who are weary and burdened and I will give you rest" (Matthew 11:28; New International Version [NIV]). I would focus on the music, the words, and playing. I gave it one hundred percent every Thursday. I was weary and tired from the caregiving and sometimes it was too much to handle, but for that hour, I let God handle all of it. At other times, as much as I could, I tried to let God handle it, but it is very hard to do that. I personally think that when you are the caregiver you need to find some way to have a little time to let God handle things for a while.

During that hour, I would get recharged. I would get rest. God was always faithful to me on Thursday mornings.

Eventually, the church canceled Thursday morning prayer due to the lack of participation. How sad it is not being able to get people to come to church and pray. I was very disappointed, but there was nothing I could do to change it.

The best part about that time was that when the Thursday morning prayer services ended, Connie was through all the surgeries and most of the health issues. She was on the road to recovery and a lot of the load was gone for me. Yes, we had a ways to go, but it was a dawning of a new day for us. It just goes to show that God knew where I was at and what I needed to make it through these trying times. I will cherish those Thursday mornings forever.

CHAPTER 13

Chemo Again?

DURING A ROUTINE FOLLOW-UP appointment, Dr. Michaels informed us there'd be a second more aggressive round of chemo for us to go through. We were in a state of shock when we heard this. Somehow we both thought it was just a one-shot deal—only one round of chemo. Neither of us was happy about it. Upon arriving home, we talked about it a lot, wondering where we had missed that part of the conversation. Anyway, the reality was that there was more to come.

Connie did a lot of research on the next chemo drug they wanted to pump into her. She did not like what she found out. The possible side effects were unsettling, the main one being lung damage. She was not at peace about this round of chemo; something about it did not sit right with her. Connie called and talked to Dr. Michaels. He confirmed that all the side effects could happen, but he said the odds of that happening to her were one in a million. After that conversation, Connie felt somewhat better, but there was still something nagging at her not to have the second round. We discussed it extensively. I told her if she was that uncomfortable with it, not to do it.

One of the biggest issues Connie had was the fact that she was a nurse and her medical background was telling her something different from what her instincts were telling her. This was a challenging battle. On one hand, her heart was saying to trust God; on the other hand, her head wanted her to go the chemo route. Again, it was the battlefield of the mind: trying to get her heart to overcome her mind. That is one tough fight.

I was not at peace with this second round either, but it ultimately came down to Connie's decision and I would respect the choice she made. I would support her completely. Knowing what she had just been through with the last round of chemo, I was unsettled by the prospect of another round.

The day for chemo arrived. Connie chose her recliner and settled in. We had a plan: Once they hooked Connie up to the pump and started the pre-fluids, I would leave and go to a local restaurant to get a couple of salads for us to eat. Salad had no smell, so it wouldn't affect those who were having chemo. A little thing like the smell of food could make someone taking chemo sick. Other patients brought food since they could be there four or more hours while the chemo was administered.

Okay, I thought, since Connie was settled in, I could leave and everything would be okay, right? Remember, the doctor had said there was only a one-in-a-million chance of something negative happening to her. I was gone about an hour. When I came around to the front of the recliner and looked at Connie, her face was beet red. She looked up at me with a look I will never ever forget. I don't know if I can explain the look. It was all in her eyes. The moment our eyes locked, I knew it was not good. "What happened"? I asked. She could barely talk, but she was able to get out, "I had a reaction to the chemo." I was speechless. The look on her face broke my heart. Dear God, NO, I thought. I immediately asked God to please help her.

Joanna quickly came over to fill me in. I found out that once the nurse hooked up the bag of chemo, she walked away. It had taken only a minute or two for the reaction to start.

Joanna wasn't Connie's nurse at the time but happened to be walking by (this was a godsend), looked at Connie, and knew something was very wrong. Connie could not talk to say anything to anyone. The chemo had started to close her throat. Joanna quickly shut the pump off and administered an antihistamine to help get things under control. By this time, they had sent for Dr. Michaels. He examined Connie and told them what to do.

By the time I arrived, they were ready to start the chemo again. I couldn't believe they wanted to restart it. They said they gave Connie enough drugs to allow her body to handle the chemo this time. The chemo was restarted with the nurse sitting right there along with Joanna. We all were staring at Connie, waiting. I was really saying prayers for Connie. After about five minutes or so, the all-clear was given: if she had not had a reaction by now, she would be okay. I continued to watch Connie like a hawk for a while. After I was convinced everything was fine, we settled down and waited for the treatment to end so we could go home.

While I was sitting there, my mind and emotions were reeling all over the place. Why did I leave? I should never have left to get dinner. I felt like I had let Connie down by not being there. If I had been there, I might have seen the reaction sooner or Connie could have gotten my attention. All I knew was I felt miserable. The battle was raging tremendously in my mind. I tried to fight the thoughts off the best I could, but it is so hard to get your mind back under control once it goes off on its own tangent. I started to pray and ask God to help get my mind under control. I knew that I had to reel it back in because Connie needed me. It was apparent we needed to talk about this when we got home and I needed to have my head somewhat clear. I told myself I had a couple of hours to get it together before the chemo was complete. I could not even imagine what was going on in Connie's mind.

One of the questions in my mind was why did they restart the chemo? To me, it made no sense that they would do such a thing after that kind of reaction. If your body rejects it, why force it to accept it? I would find this out later. But for now it was just too much to handle. It took almost the whole time the chemo was going on for me to reel my head back in with God's help. I had a conversation with God. I said, "God, this the third time I almost lost Connie, now this? I know you are protecting her, but I don't like what's happening, I don't want to lose her. Please help us." Connie and I were quiet for the most part with only a little chit chat here and there.

The chemo was finally complete and we were finally going home. We were both totally drained and emotionally spent. The next few days, we were somewhat quiet about what had happened. We talked about it a little bit, but not much, as we both had to process it. Connie started to notice that she was getting short of breath. Something like walking up the basement steps caused her to huff and puff to get to the top. We thought we would give it a little time to see if it would go away. After a few weeks it eased up some, but not a lot. Soon it was time for the second treatment.

It was decided that they would try to finish out the four sessions of chemo to help destroy any cancer that was in her body. Connie agreed to this. All I could do was support her decision. She felt she should try to complete it. When they hooked Connie up to the chemo for the second time, we all waited and watched as the chemo was pushed in; we all just stared at Connie. That must have been some sight to see. There were no issues at all. Thank God! We had done a lot of praying beforehand for this to go smoothly.

A few days later Connie's breathing got worse. Anything she did, she was out of breath. She called Dr. Michaels and we went in to see him. He said it was pneumonitis, which had been caused by the chemo. (Chapter 21 in Connie's book *The Courage to Be Imperfect* goes into a lot more detail.) He started her on prednisone to help it. This reaction to the chemo would change our lives forever.

We had to change the way we did a lot of things, even walking, because of her energy level. We had to alter our strides to a slower pace so she wouldn't get too fatigued. When you are used to walking at a regular pace and then have to change that, let me tell you, it did take some work to adjust. We had to plan where we went, so we could find places for Connie to sit and rest. We had to change our parking; we had to find places close to the door or I would drop her off at the door so she wouldn't have far to walk. Just taking a shower would wear her out some days and that would be all she'd accomplish. She would set out to get one thing accomplished for the day; sometimes she could accomplish it, and other days it would have to be done another time.

I sometimes struggled with all this, as I was trying to find the balance of doing things for Connie without making her feel helpless. We had countless conversations about how bad she felt that I had to do more. I would ask her if she could do the certain task. When she replied that she couldn't, I would tell her not to worry about it, that I could handle it. I knew that if the tables were turned, she would have done the same for me. It was just so hard for her to sit and watch. Connie also kept me in check; she would tell me if I started to smother her.

I received a phone call at work. It was Connie; she was having a lot of chest pain and needed to go to the emergency room. I immediately dropped everything I was doing and ran for the door. Thank God I lived close to where I worked. I prayed all the way home, trying to keep my feelings in check. You would think by now I would be a pro at having everything under control, but I was not.

I got Connie in the car and started to the hospital. We talked about how she was feeling but kept the conversation short because it made her short of breath. This was our first trip to the emergency room. We put Connie in a wheelchair and went inside. Once they found out it was chest pain, she was taken right back to be seen. They would not let me go back with her. There I was in the waiting room again, praying for Connie and hoping someone would come soon to let me know what was going on. I'd had about enough of these waiting rooms already. I asked God what was going on and told myself just to keep praying. I don't know how long it was before I was allowed to see Connie. Boy, was I glad when I was able to go see her.

When we were alone, she told me what had happened. She usually waited for us to be alone to talk because most of the time she did not tell them she was a nurse or they would treat her differently. She did not like that. All I can say was she was not a happy camper at all. As you read in Chapter 21 of Connie's book, the doctor was discharging her even though she was still having chest pain. I tried to calm her down.

We had to go home. Okay, here was another different emotion and situation to handle. Connie was having chest pain and was angry—not a good combination. I asked the Lord to help me say and do the right things to calm her down. It took a lot of listening for her to calm down. Her biggest issue was the doctor had not taken her seriously and was sending her home.

As a husband, how do you deal with that? There is no book or manual to say do this or do that. I was on my own—God and me. Maybe that should have been the title of this book because without Him I would have not made it at all.

As I write this years later, everyone keeps telling me to put more of what I felt into the chapters. I have thought long on this and this is what I have arrived at. When you are the caregiver and something like this happens, you go into a mental focus on what is happening. What I mean by that is, when Connie called and said she needed to go to the emergency room, the first place I went in my mind was to pray and ask God to help me because I couldn't handle this on my own. God has been faithful to me about that because I know I would be a basket case otherwise.

I had to be strong and level-headed to make decisions and to pay attention to everything happening around me. You cannot block out what is happening. It needs to be dealt with or otherwise it will be like an open wound that gets infected. At some point, you are going to have to deal with the reality of the situation. There will come a time where it will happen. Playing drums and mowing the grass was where it happened for me. I didn't have to think about mowing the grass while I was doing it, so my mind could deal with some of the things I was feeling. I also got up earlier for work to spend time with God. Psalms 63:1 says, "O God, you are my God; early I will seek you" (New King James Version [NKJV]). I knew that if I made a small sacrifice of sleep to spend with Him, He would replenish me in other ways. Try it, you might like it!

When you are the caregiver, you have to find some time for yourself just to get your head together. You need that time in order to survive. I am not suggesting you walk away and say that you need some time to yourself. Just find some time in your regular day. Here are some examples: When I would go to get groceries I would put on music in the car that I could worship God with. It might normally be only a short drive to the store, but sometimes I would take the long way home, giving me that time I needed. When you drive to work, use your time by yourself wisely. That time can be a special time for you. It is not being selfish; it is essential for your well-being. You still have to take care of yourself. I know it is hard, but you need to. If you don't, you will eventually be worn out and can't function. So try the best you can to keep yourself healthy.

Connie called Dr. Michaels and he referred her to a cardiologist because of the chest pain issue. After a lot of tests, the doctor put her on medication to help prevent it from happening again. We were on the way to recovery once again. We had a little time off from the medical stuff until… yep; you guessed it, more to come.

In April 2001, Connie was feeling pretty good, so she wanted to get out of Asheville and go away for a long weekend. We called Rose and made arrangements to spend the next weekend with her. We traveled about five hours to Rose's house. It was marvelous to get away, as we both needed it tremendously. We did not plan anything official to do. We just wanted to relax and be spontaneous. Sunday morning, Connie woke up to find her right side above her breast swollen like a balloon.

Okay, Lord, we are five hours from home. What are we going to do now? Help! Connie immediately called Dr. Donaldson's office to inform him of the situation. The doctor on call phoned in a prescription for her. He said to go home if it got worse and call back. If it didn't get worse, he'd see her when we returned. This was a new situation with a new wave of emotions to deal with.

It was not like that Thanksgiving at Connie's parents in Pittsburgh where the doctors knew her and her medical history. Here in Virginia where Rose lived, they did not know her medical history and it was complicated, as you are finding out. If we had to go to the hospital here, it would be totally trusting God to provide the right medical staff to care for her. This was supposed to be a time to get away and relax a little bit. Well, that wasn't going to happen this weekend. I wanted to head home, but Connie wanted to go to church with Rose. She insisted if it got worse, we'd head home.

The drive to church was interesting. Connie could not put the seat belt across her shoulder. She really wanted to go to church, as that would be the perfect place for her—a place with prayer.

The swelling stopped. Our weekend over, we said goodbye to Rose. On the way home, we did a lot of talking about what could have happened and we had no answers for what did happen. The trip seemed to take forever and Connie was a little uncomfortable. When we arrived home and since the swelling had stopped, she opted not to call the doctor back until the next morning.

We got an appointment and went right in. Dr. Conway said that something was leaking and the only way to find out what the issue was would be to do an outpatient surgery. It was not what we needed or wanted to hear. They scheduled the surgery for the next day. This seemed like a bad dream. The next morning, we were in the holding room waiting for them to come and get Connie. We prayed for the procedure, I kissed Connie, and off I went to the waiting room.

Once again, God and I had a lot to talk about and we did. I told Him how I was feeling and how I did not understand all this. I didn't understand how we prayed a lot for Connie and there were people all over the world praying, yet we still had to go through these issues in life. The only answer I found was that He said He would never let me go through more than I could handle. How much could we handle? I did not want to know.

The procedure did not take long. Dr. Conway came out and told me that the fluid was blood. He had found a small tear that had been the cause of the swelling, so he had cauterized the area. He said we might never know why this had occurred, that it might have happened just from her picking up something. One thing we thought of later was that Connie had forgotten to take her Barley Green with her that weekend. She was on a large amount of blood thinners. The lesson learned from this (if that was the cause of her swelling and her blood was too thin) was to make sure we had the Barley Green with us on trips away from home. After that, we took the juicer, carrots, and Barley Green whenever we traveled.

CHAPTER 14

Spinal Meningitis

IN AUGUST 2002, CONNIE's parents came down for a visit. While they were here, Connie was not feeling well. As their visit went on, I received a phone call at work from Connie informing me she was not feeling well and was having severe chest pain again. She called her cardiologist and she was told to go in right away. I dropped everything and raced home. I was blindsided by this, as I thought all that was behind us. As I drove home, I prayed that everything would be alright. I arrived home, took one look at Connie, and knew she was really feeling horrible. I got her in the car and told her parents we would call them as soon as we found out something.

At the doctor's office, they took Connie right away, hooked her up to the heart monitor, and did an EKG. We were anxiously waiting to find out what was going on. Her chest pain was subsiding, but she started getting nauseous. Before anyone could move, she began vomiting. The nurse grabbed a small trash can for her. Her temperature reached 103 degrees. The doctor came in, looked at Connie, and told her to go to the hospital. He did not even examine her, which made both Connie and me very angry. We thought he should at least examine her or do something, not just say to go to the hospital! I wanted him to help her, as she was lying on the table almost curled up in a ball. He went to call the hospital and Dr. Michaels. He came back in and informed us the hospital was waiting for us.

Connie was so sick that they gave us some bags for the trip. The hospital was only ten minutes away. On the way, Connie told me how mad she was, but she was too sick to deal with it. I prayed for her on the way there. The hospital admitted her and escorted us to her room.

I asked God what was going on. I told Him we needed a miracle here. While the staff was asking the thousand and one questions, I remembered that her parents were at our house. Oh, man, with the urgency of the situation, I had totally forgotten about them. This was something new again; how do I handle this—what do I do with her parents? I went outside the room to call them and give them an update. They were as shocked as I was that Connie was in the hospital. I told them once we got Connie settled in, I would come and get them. It was late afternoon by this point.

Back in the room, I reminded Connie that her parents were here. She was so out of it she did not understand me. They started to run every test you could think of. They also did X-rays and a scan to try and see what was going on.

While Connie was at a scan, I asked the nurse how long it would be. She said it could be a couple of hours, so I decided to go home, get something to eat, and get her parents. When I arrived home, I could tell her parents were extremely upset about what was happening with Connie. I told them after I ate something that we all would go to the hospital. They had a lot of questions for me and I answered them as best I could.

We arrived at the hospital and Connie had just gotten back from a scan. We stayed with her for quite some time. She slept a lot, even with the constant flow of nurses and doctors in and out of the room.

As I sit here writing this today, I wonder what was going through Connie's parents minds. I wonder how they felt. I called and asked them this question, but they said they could not remember. I can understand that because you have so many questions and no answers that your thoughts and emotions are all over the place. We stayed for a while and then went home. We were mostly quiet on the way home. That night, I think we were all still in shock that Connie was once again in the hospital. I did not sleep well, as I had too much running through my head. I had so many questions and not a lot of answers. I think I wrestled with God that night. I did find some peace and eventually drifted off to sleep.

We went back to the hospital the next morning and Connie was doing somewhat better. The doctors decided that Connie had a severe sinus infection, which was causing the problem. They started her on antibiotics to clear up the infection. Depending on how she was responding to the medication, she could possibly go home the following day.

With Connie's parents here, this time was more difficult for me. Previously in dealing with all the medical issues, I hadn't had to deal with anyone else being there with me. I didn't have to factor in making sure someone else was taken care of besides Connie. I would come and go as I needed to and did not have to think about someone else being hungry or tired or needing a break. The only thing I had to keep in mind was to go home, let the dog out, and feed the cat and dog. At the same time, I was not used to having someone there to talk to and having someone there with the same emotions I had. It was support in a certain kind of way I was not used to. I was very glad to have them there.

Connie was responding to the medication and was at least present and awake with us for most of the time. She still went to sleep at times while we were there. They released Connie the next day and we all went home. Connie's parents stayed the rest of that day; they decided since Connie was doing better they would go back to Ellwood City the next morning.

After Connie's parents left, she spent the remainder of the day resting. Late that evening, she started not feeling good again and her temperature was on the rise. All that night we could not get her temperature down; at one point it hit 103 degrees. We called Dr. Michaels the next morning and he wanted Connie back in the hospital. (For more details on what happened, read Chapter 23, "What a Pain," in Connie's book.)

Let the testing begin. Connie had undergone a lot of testing in the past but not like this. I think her hospital bed knew how to get to all the scan departments and to X-ray by itself. Every time the door to her room opened, someone would take her somewhere for testing. I remember this was the first time that I went and found the chapel in the hospital and prayed. God, I am asking for Your help again in letting them find out what is going on.

I do believe that God performs miracles and I know that some are spontaneous and some happen over time. I also believe that He uses doctors and medicine to heal people. He is the Creator of all things and He created medicine. So I asked God to send the right doctors and nurses and anyone else needed to provide the answers for Connie's needs.

Connie was very sick this time; she could hardly move to go to the bathroom. Again, she had hoses, tubes, and IVs hooked up everywhere they could find a vein. Dr. Michaels did a spinal tap to draw fluid out of the spinal cord so it could be tested to see if it was abnormal or not. The test showed some abnormality. Therefore, they needed more spinal fluid to do more testing since they did not have enough from the first spinal tap. Dr. Michaels did a second spinal tap to get more fluid. They discovered that Connie had spinal meningitis. They could not figure out how she got this condition; nothing was conclusive.

I had to continue going to work during all this. The only thing that helped me was that I knew she was in good hands, besides the fact that the days I was there all she did was sleep. I knew the nurses would call me if I needed to be there before my regular time to get off work. I wanted to be there in the worst way, but I had used up a lot of my time off on the other medical issues we'd had. It probably was a good thing that I worked, as it kept my mind busy, for a while anyway.

They started Connie on some high-powered antibiotics to combat this meningitis thing. The next day she was feeling better and the fever broke, but she started having severe migraine headaches. They came to the conclusion that the second spinal tap they had performed was leaking spinal fluid, so they did what is called a blood patch. Dr. Michaels took some of Connie's blood and injected it over the area where he had removed the spinal fluid. Again, it is one of those things (one in a million) that just happen.

The next day Connie was doing much better; I was so happy to see that. They finally discharged her about a week later. She was so happy to be home, but the road to recovery would be a long one for both of us. Connie had no energy at all. A good day for her was to get up and make it to the couch or computer room, if she could focus at all. I remember she could not even take a shower, as she could not stand for that long. I had to bathe her in the tub because she did not have the energy to wash herself, dry off, and put clothes on. It was hard for me to see her that way. After the first surgery, she had been weak, but nothing like this. This was so much more extensive and the recovery was going to take a lot longer than before.

I did what I could to help Connie. Before I went to work, I would make sure the phone was beside the bed, let the dog out, and get the coffee pot ready so all she had to do was push the button. Each issue we walked through together drew us closer. I think it built a massive amount of trust in each other. When you have to take care of someone to this extent, you get intimate with that person because of the care that has to be given. Some of these things are not normally done in a marriage. Connie was a very strong and independent woman; she had to take care of herself for a long time before I came along. She had a hard time letting me do things for her and letting me take care of her in this way. The last time she had tried to do things by herself, but this time she could not. So for her to trust me to this extent was a huge thing for her.

One thing about being the caregiver is that none of the care is given with strings attached—strings like "When you were sick, I had to do

_____. You owe me." I realized later on in life that this is one of the first steps to unconditional love. You may love someone, but to love them unconditionally you gladly do anything and everything for them. They are the priority.

It took a very long time for Connie to recover from this episode. Sometime after this, I was at work and someone I knew there said that she had talked to one of her customers about Connie. This person asked that we call her. She's had cancer, had gone through a double mastectomy, and was active in helping people with cancer. The person wrote her number down and I went home and told Connie about it. We called Margaret and talked to her. Connie told her a little bit about what she had gone through. Margaret said she wanted to help out in a way that we needed. She had a condo in Wrightsville Beach, North Carolina, and offered it to us so we could get away for a while. That generous offer blew us away. We took her up on her offer and a few weeks later were off to the beach.

We spent a week there walking on the beach, exploring, and taking a ton of photos. We enjoyed spending a lot of time together. One thing I loved to do was get up early and photograph the sunrise on the beach. There is a verse in the Bible that states, "Great is his faithfulness; his mercies begin afresh each morning" (Lamentations 3:23; NLT [New Living Translation])

I also spent that time walking on the beach, talking to God—just Him and me. You should try it next time you are at the beach. Get up, watch the sunrise, and talk to God; it may change your life. It was such a blessing for us to be able to escape from all our issues and medical problems for a while, not to mention the bonus of no doctors' appointments for a week!

Margaret paid us a visit while we were there. We talked for quite a while and it was nice to get to know her and thank her for this kind gift.

By the way, we found out later at a follow-up appointment what was going on with the doctor who had made us so angry by not examining Connie and just telling her to go to the hospital. He told us that when he had walked into the exam room Connie was in, he knew just by looking at her that this had nothing to do with her heart and it was more serious than that. He knew he had to move swiftly. It goes to show once again not to jump to conclusions.

The week at the beach was what was needed to give us the rest we had to have to go through the next episode of life with Connie.

CHAPTER 15

Not Again

CONNIE HAD A ROUTINE mammogram scheduled in November. She went to her appointment and had the test. While she was waiting to be released to go home after the test, the tech came in and said the radiologist wanted to see her. The radiologist said there were suspicious spots and his recommendation was to have a regular biopsy instead of a needle biopsy. This way if it was determined to be cancer, they could go ahead with a mastectomy and reconstruction. I know it was a real shocker to Connie to be told this. She had time to deal with it a little on the way home before breaking the news to me.

When Connie told me what was said, I was in disbelief, thinking once again, you have got to be kidding me! I asked her how she was doing with it. She said she was alright. "Let's just do the mastectomy and reconstruction and be done with it. That way I won't have to deal with it anymore."

Sometimes I was amazed at how she handled things, how she was able to hit things head on, deal with them, and then move on. I told her a few times she needed to write a book on everything she had been through. I got the classic "I'll think about it" response. Sometimes I think we do not take the ones closest to us seriously enough when something like that is suggested. Let's just say, she did not sit down and write.

The next thought that came to my mind was that I could not go through the surgery day alone like I had the first time. After that, what hit me was the possibility of chemo again. We were still changing our lives from the complications of chemo: breathing issues, fatigue, no energy, and more. I didn't think either of us could go through the ordeal of chemo again. God would have to step in and help. I was emotionally wiped out and drained. Just about the time I thought I had all my emotions under control and somewhat dealt with, something like this happened. It forced me to dig deeper within and dig deeper into God, letting Him lead the way and give me strength to do this again.

Connie made all the necessary doctors' appointments. Dr. Roberts, the oncology surgeon, Dr. Michaels, her oncologist, and Dr. Donaldson, the plastic surgeon, were all in full agreement on going forward with the mastectomy and reconstruction. We were told there'd be no need for chemo with the mastectomy. I was thrilled that she would not have to go through that again. We gave thanks to God for hearing and answering our prayers that there'd be no more chemo involved.

The doctors needed to get approval for the procedure from the insurance company. Here is where the crap hits the fan. The insurance company denied the request, saying they needed a letter from the doctor indicating why he felt they needed to do the mastectomy without doing a needle biopsy first. They would rather pay for a needle biopsy separately than to have it all done at the same time to make sure it was medically necessary. The plan was to schedule everything at the same time while Connie was under sedation. They would take the "hot spot" out and send it off immediately to get analyzed. If it came back as cancer, the mass would already be out and they would continue on with the mastectomy and reconstruction. It sounded simple enough to me.

Connie had an appointment with Dr. Roberts. She told him what they wanted, so he wrote the letter and sent if off to the insurance company that same day. Connie called a few weeks later to see when the surgery was scheduled only to find out that the insurance company was waiting for the letter. The ladies at the doctor's office were furious about this because the letter had been sent to the insurance company weeks before. They resent the letter to the person who Connie spoke with.

Connie waited an additional week and called again. She received the same runaround as before. She was persistent. She kept calling every week until it was taken care of. Connie also called the North Carolina Insurance Commission about it. They could not do anything but told her to call the Labor Relations Board at the federal level. The board could not do anything but told her to call the Federal Insurance Commission. After talking to several people, someone took down Connie's information and told her that because of the way the laws were written, there was not a lot they could do until the laws changed in 2003.

Connie's health was left hanging in the balance by people who had little if any medical experience. What would happen if the cancer spread? Would they be responsible for it? All this went on for the sake of money. The insurance company did not want to pay for the surgery. After three months in February, they finally approved her surgery.

I cannot imagine someone going through cancer the first time having to go through that waiting period. Connie had already gone through three bouts with cancer and I know firsthand how difficult it was for her at times. The doctors told her to keep her stress level to a minimal level if at all possible. Those three months of trying to get insurance coverage was not one of those times. It was very hard on her. We spent a massive amount of time talking it through and praying about it.

There was too much time in between all this hoopla for mind games to set in. I knew Connie was strong, but the chemo and everything involved took its toll on her. As a husband and caregiver, I was trying to do everything I could to support her. There was no book or manual to help me. I had God. He was what I had to make it through and He gave me the wisdom and guidance. I could not imagine someone who did not have God in their life being able to endure this.

I hope and pray the people on the insurance side of this never have to handle something like what they put Connie through. Both Connie and I learned a lot about forgiving people, as we attempted to forgive them. I can tell you it did take some time. Even as I write this years later, emotions start to well up inside me. I become somewhat angry for what they put us through and how they possibly endangered Connie's life. I realize I need to forgive them once again so we can move on to the next episode of life with Connie: Operation Left Side.

CHAPTER 16

Operation Left Side

THE SURGERY WAS SCHEDULED for February 12, 2002. This one would be different from what she experienced on the right side. I did not know that Connie was struggling with the feeling that she would not make it through the surgery. She was battling a lot of mind games. She never spoke about how she felt nor did she give any clue that this was what was going on for her. Personally, I think the battling she did with the insurance company took its toll on her more than I realized at the time. She was a little depressed and for her that was not a common emotion. We usually talked about everything; but this time, Connie was dealing with these things herself before she could even think of talking to me about it.

One day, Connie asked me if I wanted anyone to be with me the day of the operation. I thought about it for a little bit and said, I think I will be alright." She told me she thought I should have someone with me. I asked her why she thought that. She said she just felt like I should and she suggested that my sister Rose come. I told her it was kind of short notice for anyone to get the time off work. She had me call Rose and ask her if she could come down for the operation. Rose said she probably could but would have to ask at work tomorrow and call back. Rose called the next day and said she could come down for the operation. She would arrive the day before. Connie seemed relieved.

The day of the operation arrived quickly and we were off to the hospital once again. We checked Connie in and then were taken to the holding area. I could tell Connie was really uneasy about something. When I asked her about it, she said, "Oh, you know, the preoperational stuff." Hmm, that hadn't affected her this much before. We only had enough time to pray, kiss, and say we'd see each other later as they whisked her off to the operating room.

Rose and I trekked to the waiting room where I had previously spent a lot of time. It was wonderful to have Rose with me; I was not alone. Rose and I talked the majority of the time while the operation was in progress, catching up on life. This kept our minds occupied so I could not contemplate what was happening.

Before I knew it, Dr. Roberts walked into the waiting room and escorted Rose and me to one of the consultation rooms. He said that it was cancer, as they suspected, and they had removed all of it. They removed one lymph node as well to make sure the cancer did not spread into them. The results came back that the cancer had not spread to the lymph nodes. I was hugely relieved. I started to thank God under my breath. Dr. Roberts continued, saying he had recently read a book on how cancer patients could achieve a mindset whereby they looked at cancer as an obstacle to overcome in order to maintain a positive attitude. In his thirty years as an oncology doctor, he had never seen that—until now. Connie was the very first and only person he had known to achieve that mindset.

Wow, did that rock my world. I was speechless. I did not know what to say to that. I knew Connie was a unique person but not to this extent. Okay, I had to meditate on this a little bit.

He said Dr. Donaldson was doing his part of the reconstruction and should be finished in the next hour or so. Rose and I returned to our seats in the waiting room and began discussing what he said. A while later, Dr. Donaldson came out and escorted us to the same room. I knew this was a very good thing because, the last time, I hadn't seen him except in the recovery room. He said everything had gone very well and Connie would be in her room shortly. I was relieved a little more but not completely. That wouldn't happen until I was able to see Connie.

I finally received the phone call from the recovery room letting me know Connie was awake and would be in her room in a couple of minutes. When Rose and I arrived, the nurses were getting Connie settled in. Now I was completely relieved to see her, even though she was in and out of awareness. Rose and I stayed for a while and then left to get something to eat. We returned to the hospital and Connie was still really out of it. She wasn't able to stay awake; she would doze on and off. The nurse said I should go home to get some rest and if anything changed, they would call me. At this point, it was around 7:00 or 8:00 p.m. I kissed Connie and then Rose and I went home.

The following morning at 9:30, the phone rang with Connie on the other end asking where I was and to come get her because she was being discharged. Huh? I replied. She said, "Come and get me. I am going home." Talk about being blown away. I remember asking her if she was serious. I told her I'd be there as soon as I could. I hung up the phone and told Rose what she said. Neither of us could believe it.

When we arrived in Connie's room, she was sitting completely dressed on the edge of the bed. The first thing out of her mouth was "Did you bring donuts because I'm hungry." Huh? (I was thinking, now why would I bring donuts?) I asked if she had eaten breakfast. She said she had but was still hungry. "On the way home we are stopping for donuts," she announced.

What a difference from the first surgery. Never in a million years would I have expected this. We had figured she would be in the hospital for a few days. I asked how she was feeling. She replied, "Good, real good."

I asked if she had any pain, to which she replied, "A little bit, let's go." On the way home, we stopped by the donut shop and picked up our goodies.

Around 1:00 p.m., Connie asked Rose if she was hungry. Rose replied, "A little bit." Connie said, "Let's go get something to eat." I told them I'd go get whatever they wanted. Connie replied, "I want to go." I told her there was no way she was going after having major surgery yesterday. She said she felt good. After Rose and I tried to talk her out of it, we gave up and took her to get something to eat. We went through a drive-through so Connie wouldn't have to get out of the car. We were out for quite a while. I think we ate our way from one end of Asheville to the other. It is my personal opinion, as Connie never told me anything concerning this, but I think she was so elated the surgery went well that she had to celebrate in her own way. That drive is how we celebrated.

After Connie left the hospital, she only took one pain pill. Dr. Donaldson told Connie she had a very high pain tolerance, which he seldom sees.

A few weeks later, Connie's breast on the left side started to swell; it was getting larger on its own. When Dr. Donaldson performed the reconstruction, he put in a tissue expander rather than a permanent implant. The tissue expander had a place to inject fluid in it. Dr. Donaldson took a big needle filled with saline solution, found the port, and injected the fluid into the tissue expander until it started to stretch the skin tightly. They usually wait a week or so to let the skin expand and then do the same thing all over again until the desired size of the breast is achieved. Connie started to expand without any fluid being put in her tissue expander. Her body was producing its own fluid. Dr. Donaldson had to take the empty needle and draw a lot of fluid out. This happened several times until there was no need for him to expand it.

One month after all this took place, Dr. Donaldson did one more operation. He took out both tissue expanders and put in the permanent implants. This was a one-day procedure done as an outpatient at the medical center. We had a few more visits with Dr. Donaldson for surgery follow-up. On one visit, his nurse took us to a different room. Dr. Donaldson came in, did the usual examination, and then proceeded to lay out a lot of tools. Connie asked him what he was going to do today. He told her he was going to do the tattooing around the nipples to give them color. When he had completed that, he said he wouldn't need to see us again unless we needed him.

This was another surprise. It blew us away that we were finished. We thanked him, said goodbye, and left. In the car, we just sat there not saying anything for a while. We knew that one day it would be over, but we had not been expecting it to be today. We agreed that we needed to celebrate this milestone, so we went out for a nice dinner. We sat and talked about all we had been through. The reconstruction chapter in our lives was now complete.

Note: In the time of the first two paragraphs of this chapter, Connie was going through a lot of mind games that she was going to die. Please read Chapter 24 in Connie's book *The Courage to Be Imperfect* to discover what the battle was all about. I did not find out until sometime later what she was dealing with. When she did tell me, I was shocked and flabbergasted that she had not said anything at the time. She said she attempted to tell me, but she just could not hold it together enough to do so. Then she said she had written a letter to me explaining everything she was going through and had given it to Rose to give to me in case something did happen to her. I would understand then why she wrote the letter and could not tell me.

If I had known, I could have helped her with the battle in her mind by praying for her and letting her talk it out. What I did finally get out of her was she could not handle the pain, grief, and sadness I would have to go through in losing her. I blame the insurance company for her state of mind then; because of the extended time they took prior to the surgery, she had too much time to think and deal with things. If they had approved the surgery quickly, she would not have had to go through this mind game. When too much time elapses, no one benefits.

I had a lot of questions like why didn't you tell me? Didn't you trust me? Did you not think I could handle what you were going through?

Once I had time to process all she told me, I could understand why she did what she did. I did not hold any bad feelings toward her and I felt very good that she had taken care of what she did. It actually reaffirmed to me yet again how much she did love me. Once I figured this out, I knew I was a truly blessed man to have such a wonderful wife as Connie who truly loved me.

CHAPTER 17

Chicago

I SIT IN FRONT of my laptop on this fall day and listen to it rain. I'm at Mark's (Connie's brother's) house on his front porch, staring into space. Thank you, Mark, for letting me sit here and type, cry, and laugh. I am amazed at what one person can endure.

Connie's health continued to improve, although there was still a long road ahead of us. There is something called chemo brain. The doctor said that if it were true, it would be a one in a million chance anyone would have it. Well, guess what? She had it. Chemo brain is where the chemo affects the memory. This was no fun at all. She could not remember to do something as simple as putting the dog out or even feeding her.

I would call her in the morning and talk to her. I had to start asking questions like did you let the dog out yet? "Oh my, hang on one second," she would say, and I would hear in the background, "Do you have to go potty?" I started to let the dog out before I went to work. "Did you feed her?" I would ask. "Oh, hang on a second; let me do that right now." Her short-term memory was nonexistent. We had to leave notes on things and make lists for Connie to remember what to do. It was hard for me to watch her go through this; normally, she would not forget anything. Sometimes I felt like a nag. I did not like it one bit, but I had no choice. This lasted for quite some time and then faded away after the chemo left her body. Thank God!

After this episode with Connie, no other health issues arose. I can remember when Dr. Michaels told us that we were able to come and see him from now on only once a month, then every three months, and finally every six months. We celebrated at each of these occasions. Let me tell you, it was weird to go from having a ton of doctors' appointments in one week to having one every six months. It also saved us a lot of money and co-pays!

Connie knew that she could not go back to nursing in the hospitals as a floor nurse, so she chose to go back to school and get her degree in healthcare administration. She chose an online college and applied for an accelerated course. She did her four-year degree in two years and did so with a 4.0 grade-point average. It was a lot of hard work; when she was finished with that, she went on to get her master's degree in strategic business leadership. She also did this as an accelerated program and again earned a 4.0 grade-point average. I was so proud of her, as she worked hard to obtain these.

All this was completed over four years. In between these years, we knew our time in Asheville was coming to a close and it was time for us to move on. Asheville was the perfect place for Connie to go through these episodes of cancer because it is such an eclectic mix of people. No one cared if all you had on your head was a bandanna or a ball cap with no hair; they accept you for who you are. We were ready now to go back to big-city life. After a lot of praying, we felt the next option for our lives would be the suburbs of Chicago.

We made the decision to put our little house, which we had spent a lot of time fixing up, on the market. We knew God had His hand on this because we sold the house and moved from Asheville and bought a townhouse in the suburbs of Chicago in twenty-eight days. It was a wild ride, let me tell you! Connie was finishing up her first degree right in the middle of this. Her parents came to Asheville to help us pack and they will never know what a blessing that was. We rented a truck and my close friends from work helped us pack the truck that day. A special thanks to my coworkers for your prayers and support.

We finished packing the truck late that night and stayed in a hotel. We got up early the next morning and said goodbye to Asheville and the wonderful friends who helped, encouraged, and supported us through the cancer saga. Look out, Chicago, here we come to start another chapter in our lives.

CHAPTER 18

Settling In

OUR TRIP TO CHICAGO was nothing like the trip to Asheville. There were no issues to speak of except for a traffic jam in Indiana. We arrived about 1:00 a.m. and stayed the night in a hotel. Our closing on the townhouse we bought was scheduled for that afternoon. We met our agent, Sam, at the townhouse for a final walkthrough and then went to the closing.

Some friends in Chicago helped us move in the following day. I had been able to transfer to a job within my company, which helped a lot. It was nice not to have to look for a job. With all the cancer, Connie had to go on disability, so we had our regular income.

We were sad to leave Asheville because we had enjoyed it there, but leaving there also felt like we were leaving the cancer saga behind, making a fresh start in life, a clean slate, a new adventure. Moving to another state was no big deal for me, as my family had moved a lot over the years. At the age of two, my parents moved us from Pennsylvania to the Los Angeles area for my dad's work. He was a Master Mechanic. At that time, there was not a lot of work in Pennsylvania for him. His brother moved to California first, then called my dad and told him he had a job for him that would almost double his salary. So we packed everything up in the truck and left for California to begin a new life. That event led me to move from coast to coast.

There were a few things Connie and I had to deal with: Connie had no doctors in the Chicago area. We knew we had to at least find a family doctor to start with. We decided that every six months we would travel back to Asheville and go see all of her doctors over a long weekend. That would give us some time to find an oncologist here in Chicago.

Our townhouse was in the suburbs twenty miles or so out of Chicago. It needed some cosmetic work but no major renovations. We did a few things like paint walls, worked on one of the bathrooms, put new flooring in the kitchen, and replaced the bannister going upstairs.

Connie's parents came for a visit. Connie tried to talk her dad into building a mantel for the fireplace, but he did not want to; he was more interested in the bannister. Did I hear the word help? Oh yeah, I jumped all over that one because Connie's dad was very good at woodworking. We picked up most of the materials beforehand so we'd have them when we were ready to begin. It was a lot of fun doing this project with Connie's dad. We were able to get most of it completed before they went back to Pennsylvania.

Connie's health continued to improve over this time. We made a few trips back to Asheville for all the doctors' appointments. At every visit, the doctors were very pleased with her progress. The breathing was still an issue for her, along with her stamina. We adjusted our lives around this to keep moving forward. I continued to work and Connie was able to keep up with most of the housework. One thing that really zapped her energy was to vacuum, so I would do that, along with most of the cleaning that required harsher chemicals such as cleaning the tub in the bathroom, as the fumes would affect Connie and her breathing.

Connie continued her schoolwork and she wanted me to go back to school to get a degree as well. I knew I needed to do that, but I wanted to wait until Connie was finished with her degree and working again before I would start on mine. I also did not want to create too much debt, as we were still paying on doctors' bills.

We spent some time exploring our new area. Two trips downtown were memorable: the Navy Pier and the Art Institute of Chicago. The food in the area was always very good. We learned from the locals great places to eat and where not to eat. We learned a lot from our good friends that lived downtown at that time as well.

We had to make a big adjustment to the Chicago winter, as it was bitterly cold! I had to be at work at seven and sometimes the roads would be really icy not to mention the amount of snow and the speed with which it came down. When it was extremely cold or frigid outside, Connie had to remain inside, as it was hard on her breathing. So on days when it was nice outside, she was eager to get out of the house and run errands or go shopping.

On one of our trips to Asheville to see the doctor, Connie talked to Tina, Dr. Michaels' physician's assistant. They were discussing Connie's breathing when Connie mentioned something about the stairs in the house. If Connie made a lot of trips up and down the stairs during the day, she would be exhausted. She spent a lot of time on the computer upstairs in the study, so if she needed anything in the kitchen or to take anything to the washer and dryer, it was the stairs again. I would haul the laundry up and down the stairs on laundry days and she would use the laptop downstairs. Connie would have to plan every trip downstairs to make sure she would get everything she needed in order to lessen the number of trips she'd have to make. Tina suggested getting a ranch-style house, as they have no steps. This made so much sense that we wondered why we hadn't thought of it. Our house in Asheville had been ranch-style, and the only thing in the basement was the washer and dryer. That started us thinking about looking for another place to live, getting something on one level.

After a long period of searching, we found a ranch-style house we liked. After a couple of years at the townhouse, we sold it and moved into our new home.

About the middle of 2006, we had moved into our house and life was going really smoothly for us. Connie was doing great. The only issue was that the house we had moved into was farther from my work, which made my commute longer. I was looking to transfer to new locations that were being built; however, it would be a six-month wait before one of the locations closer to home would be opened. When that happened, my commute would go from an hour and a half to twenty minutes.

Our house did not need any work except for painting, and that was not an issue because both Connie and I enjoyed painting. It was nice to have everything all on one level again, which made a big difference for Connie; she was not as tired in the new house.

We started to find a few doctors for Connie in Chicago, but we did not want to stop seeing Dr. Michaels. So we continued to drive to Asheville when it was time to see him. Connie had to find a cardiologist in Chicago; after some research, she found one. She got established with him after a few visits and after some testing he decided that Connie did not need to continue taking her heart medication; it wouldn't harm her at all. He said he would leave that decision up to her. Connie decided to quit taking the medication, and her heart was given a clean bill of health. Wow, thank you, God! What a blessing. It surely was a miracle. We went out that night to our favorite restaurant and celebrated. You have to celebrate these moments in life; it is important to remember to do that.

Life was good once again. There was hope. Blessings were here and there: my job, Connie's health, a new house, and Connie was finishing up her master's degree. There was some breathing room again where we could almost relax for a bit and enjoy life. This had been a rare thing for us.

It was now over five years of Connie being cancer free. That is what the medical field said was the time span from the last episode of cancer. A four-time cancer survivor was rare and my wife was the person who had beaten all the odds. I was a very blessed man indeed.

Connie finished up her master's degree and, feeling good, wanted to return to work. She knew she could not pursue nursing; she would have to do office work of some kind. Social Security provided a person to help Connie find a job. They worked together and Connie had a few job interviews, but they were not right for her. She was happy to be looking for a job; it was unreal. Disability would let her work for a while, stop paying her, and if she found she could not work, they would restart the benefits. The search was on.

While this was going on, we were finishing up Connie's book, *The Courage to Be Imperfect*, getting it ready to publish (more about this in Chapter 20). With the final touches complete, we were able to get the book published. Life was very good indeed. Things were falling in place for us after such a long battle.

We were able to enjoy this feeling for a few days—until a trip to the emergency room set the stage for the Fifth Time.

CHAPTER 19

The Fifth Time

I SIT IN FRONT of my laptop gazing at the title, then find myself staring into space contemplating how to start this chapter. Life sure does throw you curve balls. Yep, you are reading it correctly: number five.

We had been toiling approximately five years on *The Courage to Be Imperfect*. A massive amount of labor went into the book. We chose the self-publishing route due to the expense of a publisher. We executed everything: all the cover work, the majority of the editing, formatting the pages, and so on. After receiving a few copies back from the printer and reviewing it with a fine-tooth comb in what seemed like a million times, Connie was ready to launch her book. We had waited so long for this day to arrive. We hopped online to the website, logged in. Ready? Connie clicked the mouse button. The cursor was on the publishing your book button. Click, you are now an author of a book you have worked so diligently on your entire life.

We were so excited that we called everyone we knew. Wow, it was finally complete. We purchased an extra package to assist us in marketing her book for websites like Amazon, Barnes and Noble, all the major book sites. Connie's entire goal for her book was to help and encourage people on their journey through cancer. It was a totally monumental day.

Now let me go back in time a few weeks before to August 20, 2007. Connie was not feeling very well. She was having a difficult time catching her breath, no matter what she did, whether it was walking across the room, talking, anything. She called her general doctor, explained what was happening, and was told to come right in. After the doctor examined her, she decided to admit Connie immediately into the hospital to run further tests.

The nurses got her settled in her room, we answered the thousand and one questions they had, they started some IVs (I think it must be a hospital law somewhere to stick you with needles and start IVs as soon as possible), and the testing began. The doctor ordered a barrage of tests and X-rays. They checked everything and could not find any explanation for Connie's breathing problem. Her breathing returned to normal after a couple of days, so she was discharged pending follow-up with a few doctors.

A week or two later, Connie had the follow-up appointment with Dr. Pete, a pulmonologist. We discussed many things concerning what could have been the problem and he wanted to try some other drugs. At the end of the visit, he told Connie that he had looked at the X-ray of her chest and saw something on the bones he didn't like. He told her she needed to see her oncologist.

Connie was still seeing Dr. Michaels every six months, along with most of the other doctors. He knew her health history better than anyone else and he had been through so much with her. She consulted with Dr. Michaels and he and Dr. Pete agreed that Connie should find an oncologist in Chicago. After a lot of research, she decided on Dr. Dan. Dr. Michaels said he would still help out in any way he could.

Back home in Chicago, the first appointment with Dr. Dan was a new patient visit during which a lot of information and blood work was required. He also wanted CT scans to get an accurate picture of what was happening. The scans were completed and the next appointment was scheduled.

We were optimistic about everything that was taking place. We spent a large amount of time praying about it. We only told a couple of people about what was going on. We did not tell any family members because we wanted to wait until we had more information to give them. We believed it would be nothing. We tried not to jump to any conclusions. The day of the appointment was an anxious time, but we kept our faith high as we entered the doctor's office.

After going over the results of the scans, Dr. Dan stated that Connie had previously had breast cancer three times. This was now the fourth occurrence for breast cancer and a total of five times of having cancer of any type. He said this one had metastasized to the bones.

We were speechless. It was like someone hit us with a baseball bat in the gut really hard. (Side note: I do not know how doctors do this day in and day out. Let me tell you, they are very special people.) Obviously, this was not what we wanted to hear. Dr. Dan stated that it was treatable with chemotherapy, which was not a word I wanted to hear. They could also give her a drug called Zometa to strengthen her bones. He had considered radiation, but Connie's body had already gone through all it could from that treatment previously, so it was not an option.

This was a lot to digest. We did not make any decisions right then, as we needed some time to handle this. There was way too much to process. It was a quiet ride home—what could we say? It had been over five years since Operation Left Side. Now the cancer was back. Once again, I was shaken to the root core of who I was. I would have to dig deeper inside myself than I had ever dug before. I did not think I had anymore in me; I'd had somewhat of a rest for five years. Now this.

I could not pray for a while. I still listened to praise and worship music and I also had my drums set up in the basement. Some days those drums took a real beating. I was angry with God—how could You let this happen again? Don't you think four times is enough? When I was able to pray, there were some interesting prayers. One thing about God is He will let you be totally honest with Him; He will listen to you. I know I needed to get everything I was feeling off my chest. I knew I had to do that to move on. I knew God was my lifeline and I had to get the lines of communication open once again from my end. He was waiting for me to deal with it.

The real kicker to this was that we were informed about the bone cancer only a day or two after Connie clicked the mouse button to publish her book.

CHAPTER 20

The Courage to Be Imperfect

WHEN DR. ROBERTS STATED that Connie had a mindset he'd only read about and not seen, it struck a chord in Connie. As the surgery she was recovering from was less complicated than the others, she had time to dwell on his statement. We talked a lot about her writing a book. It was hard to believe that anyone could go through so much and keep such an awesome attitude, never having the self-pity party, and never really asking the question "Why me?"

We were talking one day about her writing her book and Connie said, "I have no desire to do the physical writing of a book nor do I have the energy to do that." I thought about it for a moment and said, "Have someone else put it down on paper for you." She said she'd never thought about that idea. I told her to find out if Mark, her brother, would want to help her with it, as he wanted to be a writer and reads a massive amount of books. Connie loved the idea. She and Mark had always been really close and he knew her almost better than anyone else. Connie called Mark to ask him if he wanted to help her write her book. Mark immediately said yes and thought it was a great idea. "No one we know has ever gone through cancer four times and overcome it," he said. The biggest issue with this arrangement was we lived in two different states: We were in North Carolina and Mark in Pennsylvania. How were we going to do this? A lot of brainstorming brought forth the idea: Connie would talk into the microphone attached to the computer and record her story. Then she'd put it on a CD and send it to Mark. Once Mark received it, he would listen to it, and then put what Connie spoke onto paper. This was no easy task for Mark to complete; it took hours to do that. He would listen to a sentence and then put it on paper; sometimes he had to rewind and listen again to get what she was saying. Connie would explain in detail and elaborate on the medical terms and procedures that took place. Sometimes Connie would change thoughts in an instant; Mark had to listen to that train of thought, and then in the next moment Connie would realize she was on a "rabbit chase." She would giggle and try to bring the thoughts back together. It was a long process for both of them, as there were thirteen discs in total.

Connie would spend some time in preparation, jotting down thoughts and details she wanted to complete in the next disc she would record. There were some days that she would hit a wall or resistance. We talked about it and we came up with the idea (another God moment) to play praise and worship music in the background really soft so the microphone would not pick it up. It set the atmosphere for the time she spent recording. We also spent a great deal of time in prayer beforehand to help out.

When we did all this, the difference it made for her was extraordinary. Sometimes you have to change the atmosphere; you need to change the sound. It relates to when you want to have a romantic dinner: You put out candles, nice china, good silverware, and soft romantic music. You would not want to play rock music, as that would change the atmosphere and make everything wrong. I hope you can get my drift! When you are not having a good day, change the atmosphere.

I can recall the day Mark called and said he had the first chapter completed; Connie was so excited she called me to the phone. We put it on speakerphone and Mark proceeded to read the chapter to us. Here Connie and I were in our very small kitchen, leaning on the counter, staring at the cradle of the phone base, not moving, trying not to make a sound so we would not miss anything. Mark finished reading and we were both blown away at what he had written; to hear Connie's life being read was incredible. She and Mark were on their way.

We had no idea what was involved in writing and publishing a book. We did a lot of research and read books on the subject. We had some time before the writing had to be completed; Mark worked on the book as he got extra time because he had a full-time job. As he completed the chapters, he emailed them to us. Every once in a while there would be a statement he had added and embellished about what Connie had done as a kid. She would read it and it would take her by surprise. "That is not true, that is not the way it happened!" she would exclaim. In the next instant, she would pick up the phone and call Mark, saying, "You have this statement all wrong," and proceed to tell him the way it happened. Mark would start laughing as Connie went on. Then she would realize that he had done this on purpose. "Oh, you just wait until I see you! This is not funny at all," she said. That would make Mark laugh even harder. He got away with it a few times before she caught on to what he was doing. I will never forget those moments.

It took a couple of years to complete the writing. Every so often we would make a trip to Mark's house so he and Connie could go over what was written and make changes as needed. It was always a fun time to listen to them being serious for a long time and then one of them would make a wisecrack about something. The moment would be lost, so it would always turn into coffee time! The time they spent in writing her book drew them closer together. They were always close, but this took it to another level.

Once Connie and Mark completed the chapters, Connie enlisted the help of her sister Nancy to do some of the editing of the book. Nancy went over the book, and had Connie and Mark add more to the chapters, saying, "You need to expand this chapter; you are not giving enough information." One thing Connie was trying to do was get her story out about being a four-time cancer survivor and then release a second book about the inner workings of the mindset she had. She wanted to go into a lot more detail in the second book; she was trying to find the balance of how much information to give in the first one. Connie was a very private person; sometimes she had a hard time letting go and giving the information. We discussed some of the specific scenarios that could take place, like if someone wanted to interview you, how much would you tell them? People want details on what you went through.

Nancy would email Connie a chapter with notes on what she thought it needed. Connie would do what she felt was needed and send it back to Nancy. Toward the end of Nancy completing her work, we made a trip to Pennsylvania. I left after the weekend to return to work, but Connie stayed for the week, working with Mark and Nancy to finish up and brainstorm on what was needed to complete the book. This was around the time we made the move from Asheville to Chicago.

Connie's book was nearing completion as far as the writing went. The next thing we had to think about was a publisher. Connie did a lot of research on this. Most publishers would not receive a manuscript from the author; they wanted an agent to present it to them. After talking about it, we chose to go the self-publishing route. Once again Connie spent a tremendous amount of time on the internet researching self-publishers, and after narrowing it down, we finally found one we were satisfied with. We signed up and started to look into what was needed to get it ready to publish. Connie came to a decision on the title: *The Courage to Be Imperfect.* Connie felt that title was fitting for her. To go through all this took a lot of courage and, yes, she was imperfect from it all, but it was okay not to be perfect.

Nancy finished her part and emailed the book back to Connie who went over it with a fine-tooth comb. We paid for an editor to go through her book. We choose one that was listed on the publishing website. Connie made all the arrangements and emailed her manuscript to the editor.

What an anxious time this was, not knowing what they would think about her book. Of course, we as family thought it was perfect. There were different levels of editing you could choose from: basic to pick it apart or tear it up. Connie chose the latter one because she wanted the book to be right. A few weeks, later we received the manuscript back from the editor. Finally, the moment of truth arrived. In her email, she commended Connie on an outstanding job on her book. She said her story was awe-inspiring and, as far as the editing, she did not need to do that much; there were some little things that needed to be fixed, but that was it. Connie was to fix everything and send it back to her, which she did. We received it back in about a week with an email from the editor stating it was done. She also said that we had paid to have it "picked apart," but she had not needed to do much editing, so she wanted Connie to choose a charity where that money could be donated.

We had to do the front cover and the back of the book as well, which was a process all in itself. Connie had an idea of what she wanted the cover to look like. She wanted one of our photographs on the cover and she knew which one. It was one of a sunrise I had taken on the beach at St. Augustine, Florida. I love to get up early when we are at the beach and take photographs of the sunrise and spend time with God. This photograph she chose we had entitled "Hope." We had named the photo before she started on the book. We had to name our photographs in order for them to be copyrighted.

Connie wanted me to design the cover. She told me what she wanted and I kept working on it until we came up with what Connie had in mind. The publishing website gave us templates to work with; everything had to be correct. We felt we had the cover right, so we moved onto the inside of the book. We had to get all the pages correct; boy, that was no easy feat. It was not easy getting all the margins and the spacing lined up. We finally felt like we had everything correct, so we submitted it to the publisher. They looked at it to make sure it was in the parameters required for printing. Once they approved the book, one copy would be printed and sent to us to preview in order to make sure it was what we wanted. This copy was free; there would be a charge for additional copies.

It seemed like quite a while for the first copy to arrive at our house, but it was actually only a week or two. I received a phone call from Connie one day telling me the book was here. She was very excited and happy—almost five years in the making and she had a copy of her book in her hands. We went out to dinner for a celebration at our favorite restaurant. When we got home, she called almost everyone we knew to let them know her book had arrived.

We went over her book and there was still some work to be done. There were little things we needed to fix: a few grammar errors, the cover needed to be tweaked, the margins, and so on. We had to get a few more copies printed every time we submitted the corrected project to be printed. The last time, we went over the copy, liked it, and found no problems, so Connie was finally able to publish her completed book, *The Courage to Be Imperfect*.

CHAPTER 21

ONJ Jaw Death

CONNIE BEGAN HAVING PAIN in her right side around her hip, making it uncomfortable to sit for any period of time. She would constantly have to shift around in the chair or wherever she was sitting to find a better position. Sometimes she would have to get up and walk around. When she did that, she could sit back down and it would be okay for a while. Additionally, she would take Tylenol and that would usually handle the pain.

The pain started to get worse. When Connie lay down in bed on her right side for any length of time, she would get nauseous and have to move and roll over. If she didn't wake up and move or roll over, she would eventually vomit. At her appointments with Dr. Dan, she would tell him about the pain that was going on. He examined her and didn't find anything. Not long after that, he ordered a CT scan to check how well the chemo was working on the cancer. Connie told him she couldn't lie still for that length of time; she would have to move around. While you are in the CT scan machine, you have to lie completely flat and still for a half hour or better. She couldn't do it. Dr. Dan also ordered the CT scan to see why she was having the pain and getting nauseous. Finally, in one of the appointments, I don't know whether it was Connie or the doctor's suggestion, but they decided to give her a small dose of Ativan to see if that would help her lie flat and still long enough to get the CT scan completed. The Ativan would assist with that. They ended up doing the scans in parts. We would have to schedule another appointment and come back to get the scan completed.

Soon the pain started to go along the right side of her ear toward the bottom of her jaw, which was very painful for her. If it was that uncomfortable for Connie, it was severe. Connie could tolerate a massive amount of pain. I stated in the earlier chapter that, after a mastectomy and reconstruction, she only took one pain pill and didn't take another one after that. So for her to say it was hurting, it had to be excruciating, and I could see on her face that it was.

This was another time when, as a caregiver and husband, there was nothing I could do to help but pray. And I can tell you, I prayed. We prayed together and we had people around the world praying for Connie. As I write this, I take a minute to reflect. All we had were faith and hope, which were the core of our existence. I sit here, shaking my head, running through in my mind all those experiences, and I am amazed by what Connie went through and how strong she stood in her faith.

Back to our story...

Dr. Dan suggested that Connie go see a neurologist, as they were thinking that her current problems had something to do with the nervous system. They suggested one particular doctor and we made an appointment for late in the afternoon so I could get time off from work and go with her. We arrived for the appointment, signed in, sat down, and waited. An elderly gentleman came out and called Connie's name and we followed him back to the office. The office was small and kind of cluttered. The elderly gentleman sat down at a desk. There were two chairs; one was close to the desk that Connie sat in and I sat in the other one. The elderly gentleman introduced himself as the doctor. I don't remember his name. We were both surprised, because out of all the doctors' appointments we had been to, the doctor had never come out himself to get the patient. I could tell by Connie's expression that did not sit well with her.

The elderly gentleman sat there asking the ten thousand and one questions about her history. When they got through that, he looked at her and said, "So what is your problem?" I was stunned by that question and I could tell that Connie did not like that at all. From that point on, the appointment went downhill, but we were there so we had to continue on. He examined her and said he didn't know what was causing the pain. His suggestion was to do a spinal tap. He was hoping that the fluid retrieved from the spinal tap would reveal why there was pain and what was happening to cause the issue. The doctor wanted to schedule this spinal tap right then and there, but Connie stated that she wanted to go home to think about it and get back to him. I knew right then and there that there was not going to be a spinal tap.

We left the appointment, got back in the car, and proceeded home. We talked about the appointment and everything that had transpired, and we agreed that we did not like the way it had gone. So it was back to the drawing board to find another neurologist.

Connie called Dr. Dan's office and told him that she did not care for what had transpired and was not comfortable with it, and asked him for another referral. He suggested another neurologist and they tried to get Connie an appointment, but she was so booked up that it would be three weeks away. They made the appointment and we had to wait.

While we were waiting for the appointment, Connie was still having a lot of pain, so the doctor gave her some stronger pain pills to help. Connie had a dentist appointment for a routine visit and they found a tooth that needed a crown and a root canal. A crown and root canal is something we did not need right now, but it had to be done. Our dentist did not do the root canal, so we had to go to a specialist to get that done. He only did crowns. As most of you know, the crown is not done in one appointment. You go for the first appointment, they grind the tooth off, prepare it for the crown, and then they make a temporary crown to put on until the original is made. Connie thought that she could sit through a crown replacement without any Ativan. She went to this appointment by herself, since she wasn't taking any Ativan. She could drive so she thought everything would be okay and she could handle it. Well, at the very end of the procedure, Connie needed to switch positions and she couldn't. She got the dentist to stop and luckily they had a trash can nearby and she vomited. She was absolutely mortified. She was able to rinse her mouth out and he was able to finish the procedure. It really bothered her that this had happened, so when she made the appointment to go back and have the crown put on, I went with her so she could take some Ativan. She did not want that to happen again.

Dr. Dan wanted to do a PET scan to check the progress of the remission of the cancer. They had just received a new PET scan machine, which was supposed to give a better view of the body. They knew the PET scan had to be done in two sessions. Connie and I went to the appointment. The building where the PET scan machine was had a nice big waiting room. As I was sitting there waiting for Connie to come back from the scan, I noticed there were different people going around from person to person and talking to them. One lady made her way to me, introduced herself, and asked if she could sit down. When I said yes, she sat down and told me she was a volunteer and what they did for the people who were in the waiting room until the patient came back out. She was offering a free hand rub to help relax the people in the waiting room. I thought that was very nice of her to offer that and the hand rub did actually help relax me.

The next person who made her way to me asked if there was anything she could do for me. I told her I was okay. She asked a few questions about why I was there and for whom I was waiting, so I took advantage of the moment and told her some of Connie's story. I blew her away with all that

Connie went through and what I went through with her. We talked for another minute or two, and then she asked if she could pray for me. During all that Connie and I went through, not many people asked if they could pray for me. This wonderful lady in the waiting room went from person to person, talking to them and praying for them. This particular lady made my day and I thank God for her. I am grateful for that moment of time she cared enough to pray for Connie and me.

Connie came out from the PET scan. I could tell by the look on her face that something was wrong. When we got to the car, she told me what had happened. Right in the middle of the scan, Connie had all of a sudden gotten nauseous and vomited in the machine. Again, she was so mortified that this had happened and there were no answers as to what was going on. I can see how God in His infinite wisdom had this lady praying for Connie and me, because little did we know what was going on with Connie in the PET scan machine; again, all we have is faith and hope.

The scan would have to be completed at the second session so we went home. In the meantime, it was time for the appointment with the neurologist. She was excellent. She talked to Connie, asked a lot of probing questions, and examined her. At the end of appointment, she told Connie she didn't think it had anything to do with her nerves or the nervous system; it had to be something else. That wasn't too reassuring to us, but at least we were fairly confident that it had nothing to do with the nervous system. The doctor suggested that the next time they did a scan to have it done at the hospital and just put Connie under anesthesia so they could complete the scan and Connie wouldn't have to go through everything she'd been through. Wow! Why didn't somebody else think of that? Oh well, at least somebody did. Needless to say, the next time a scan was due, it was done in the hospital, they administered anesthesia, and she came through with flying colors.

Eventually, the pain in her hip and her leg started to subside, but the pain in her jaw traveled from her right ear down to the center of her bottom jaw and was, at times, excruciating. Connie noticed that her bottom gums were loosening along her teeth. Not long afterward, a few of her bottom front teeth became loose. Once again, she made dentist appointments and talked to doctors and nobody seemed to have a clue as to what was happening.

We had to move back to Pennsylvania even though she was still having pain in her jaw, and the saddest part about this is we had to find all new doctors for her (more about this in Chapter 23). About seven or eight miles from where we lived in Pennsylvania, there's a quaint little town called Zelienople. Connie found out about a specialist in dentistry there.

To our amazement, in our first or second appointment, this dentist told Connie that she had osteonecrosis of the jaw, or ONJ jaw death, and that it is a side effect of the drug Zometa, which causes the jaw tissue around the teeth to shrink. Dr. Dan had put Connie on that drug to help strengthen her bones. At the time, we thought it was a good idea because, with the breast cancer being metastasized to the bone, it would counteract the cancer. The drug had been administered along with the chemo.

"We see this all the time in cancer patients that are receiving Zometa," the dental specialist said. Finally, somebody who knew what was going on! In this sleepy little town, this particular doctor knew what was happening. Why it is that no one in the Chicago area had a clue as to what was going on? I guess that's a question we will never know. They stopped administering the Zometa and, a few months after that, her pain went away.

In July 2009, Connie was in the hospital after losing a bottom tooth. I can remember going to the hospital after work, walking in the room, and just seeing the look on her face, I knew something was wrong. "I lost another tooth," she said. My heart broke once again—why does this have to happen? I know now that there are no answers to the questions you ask. You can ask "Why? Why? Why?" all you want, but all you end up having is faith and hope.

CHAPTER 22

ER Episode Two

CONNIE HAD NOT BEEN feeling well for a day or two. Again, she was short of breath, her heart was racing, and she tried everything she knew to get it back to normal. I had gone to work. She knew to call me if she needed me. I also called her a couple of times a day to talk to her and make sure everything was alright. This particular morning, the shortness of breath became worse, so she called her pulmonologist who told her to come right in. Connie called me at work and told me she had to go see him. I told her I would be right home, as I was twenty minutes away. She said I did not need to come home because she was okay to drive herself. She also added that it was no big deal.

Something inside me said don't let her go by herself. It was the still small voice of God. I said I will be home in twenty minutes so get ready and I will take you because I am not comfortable with you going alone. We had such trust in each other that when one or the other said something like that, we did not question it.

We arrived at the doctor's office and they took Connie right into one of the exam rooms. The nurse came in and did all the routine things, asked a ton of questions, then said the doctor will be in shortly. Dr. Pete came in looking at the chart, and then he started to examine her, asking questions. After a few minutes, he said we needed to admit her to the hospital; he wanted her to go directly to the emergency room.

The doctor's office was attached to the hospital through an annex. He said, "I will be right back." He was gone only a minute or so. He opened the door and pushed in a wheelchair! "Okay, here you go. The nurse is on the phone with the ER right now. They will be expecting you." We put Connie in the wheelchair and off we went. We followed the hallways, which had colored lines leading you to the emergency room.

When we arrived at the emergency room, a nurse asked who we were and, upon our reply, wheeled Connie right in, as they were ready for her. They put her on the bed and several nurses appeared out of nowhere. One was on the computer and started to ask Connie all kinds of questions. Before I knew it, they had Connie attached to several monitors and the IVs were flowing once again. I was standing off to the side, taking it all in and answering any questions I could. Connie's heart rate was really fast.

The on-call cardiologist decided to give Connie a drug that would stop her heart for a few seconds and then the heart would start back up again. I was not too crazy about it, but what they were trying to do was break the rhythm of the heartbeat so when the heart started back up, it would beat to its normal rhythm. It was one of the weirdest things I had seen. Once they gave Connie the drug, everyone stopped what they were doing, everything got really quiet, and all the medical staff stared at the monitor, waiting. Her heart stopped. After a few seconds, someone said it should start about now. Her heart restarted and resumed with the same fast rhythm. After trying several things, nothing seemed to slow the heart down, so they admitted her to the cardiology floor.

As for me, the whole time spent in the emergency room was a blur; things happened so fast. The staff was on top of their game in the ER; it was extraordinary to see in real life. I watched and listened as things happened, trying to pray, but there was so much going on. We had to wait for the drug to do its thing, and I prayed hard for Connie during that time. I also prayed for the staff that God would help them to find out why this was happening a second time.

Once we arrived on the cardiology floor, we were taken to her room. The rooms were all private rooms, so we both liked that. Oh boy, here we went again with the ten thousand and one questions that every new nurse had to ask.

In watching everything that was going on, my mind was racing with what seemed like a million thoughts: God, what is going on again? Why is she going through this? Are you trying to teach us something? There was no answer. God was silent once again. All you can do once again is to trust that He is in control and will take care of everything. Sometimes that is not comforting at all. You want Him to say in His big deep God voice that everything will be alright. I am right here. Do not worry. You want that physical touch, but what you have instead is a sense inside you knowing He is there.

They started Connie on an IV drip to break the rhythm. The nurses got Connie settled in. They had her on the monitor, so they could watch her from the nurses' station. Finally, I had some time alone with Connie to talk to her. She told me that she had not liked the drug they gave her in the emergency room. She said it was the weirdest feeling to feel your heart stop and start back up again; she could feel it all. She told me to never let them give that to her again. She also chuckled and said, "Good thing I didn't drive myself. I thought I could, but now I am so glad I didn't."

Her heart rhythm finally broke that night and went back to normal. Connie was in the hospital for a few days just to make sure everything was alright. They ran the full gamut of tests to try and find out why this had happened; they did a lot of X-rays and scans. They could not find the cause of this heart rhythm issue.

Connie was to be released on a Saturday. I had to be home because our house was for sale and we had planned an open house with the realtor. We did not want to cancel it, as this had been in the works for a while and we needed to sell the house to move back to Pennsylvania (more in the following chapter). I spent most of the day that Saturday getting the house ready, doing things like cutting the grass, cleaning the house, and straightening up. Why had this happened now? Connie was in the hospital, we needed to move, I was at home working on the house, and I needed to be at the hospital with Connie. I knew she was doing better since her heart rate was normal again and her breathing was under control. Life really stinks at times. Cancer—I really hate it. I hate what it does, not only to the person, but also to the whole family. It changes life forever.

I finally had the house close enough to what it needed to be for the open house, so I went back to the hospital. Connie looked so much better that it made me feel better. Connie was telling one of the hospital staff about her book and telling some of her story. I chuckled to myself and thought, yes, she is feeling a whole lot better! They were ready to discharge her, so I helped Connie get ready to go home

We could not go home for a few hours because of the open house, so after being discharged from the hospital, we went to get her prescriptions and, while waiting for them to be filled, sat in the car talking about everything that had happened over the past few days. We also talked about what I had accomplished with the house and wondered how many people had showed up for the open house. We started driving back home when there was only a half hour or so until the open house was to end. Our realtor reported that it had gone well. A few people were interested and would make an offer. The realtor left and we were finally able to relax for a while. Over the next few days, Connie returned to her normal self or what was normal for her.

CHAPTER 23

Back to Pennsylvania

CAN I SAY IT one more time? I hate cancer! When we had purchased the new house in Chicago, cancer was not part of the plan. We were doing well. Connie was looking for a job. I was actually looking into going back to school. Then that dreaded word I heard too many times—cancer—reared its ugly head yet again. The medical bills started to roll in. We had a co-pay of thirty-five dollars every time we walked in the door for a scan or a doctor's appointment. We did not have enough money to pay everything. Connie had to have all the scans, doctors' appointments, and medications, so we had to make a tough choice, which was to sell the house and move somewhere.

We talked a lot about what to do and where to go. This was at the top of our prayer lists; we spent a lot of time praying about this. It came down to three choices: One option was to sell the house and stay in the Chicago area and find a much smaller place. The second option was to sell the house and move to Pennsylvania where we would be near Connie's family, and the third option was to sell the house and move to Virginia to be near my family.

We looked around at different houses in different areas in Chicago, but that was turning out not to be an option because it was too expensive and selling and buying another house was like exchanging money; even renting was not an option. It came down to either Pennsylvania or Virginia. We discussed it at length. I was leaning to Virginia, and Connie was leaning to Pennsylvania. Connie was adamant about going to Pennsylvania. I do not know this for sure, but I think Connie knew more than what she was telling me about why she wanted to go to Pennsylvania. One statement she made over and over again was that there her family could help me more with the appointments and whatever else we needed. In Chicago, I could not go to a lot of her doctor's appointments like I did in Asheville. The decision was made by both of us that we would go to Pennsylvania, get through this episode of cancer, and move on from there.

Connie was doing much better with this episode; the chemo and a lot of prayer were working. By the time we left Chicago in June 2008, her tumor markers were down. Her doctors were not happy about us moving, but we had no choice. Now the work began. We had to find a realtor to sell the house, and start looking for houses to rent in Pennsylvania. Connie called her family and told them that we were moving back. They were excited to have Connie come back home.

We found a realtor and put the house on the market. Now it was the waiting game for a buyer. We also put my corvette up for sale, which I'd had since 1983. We always thought that we would get it on the road and do a few car shows. I knew it was time to sell it. Connie did not want to sell it but left that decision to me. I knew this would pay a few bills and pay for our move to Pennsylvania. The car sold quickly, which was a blessing. We now had a little extra money, but we needed to be careful and wise with it.

We had some showings on the house but no offers. If this book had audio, you could hear Connie's animation in telling the following story. Connie was working on her second book and had a small tape recorder that she would talk into so she would not lose her thoughts. We had a showing scheduled for 2:00 p.m. The realtor showed up an hour early with the client in tow. There was a mix-up on the time they were to arrive. Connie was not ready for them. The toilet had backed up in the guest bathroom. Connie had the new toilet plunger out with all its adaptors; she had started to clean up but was not finished yet. She also needed to change clothes; she was in her sweatpants and sweatshirt. Connie answered the door and found out it was the realtor. She told them they could not come in yet, as she was not ready for them. She told them she needed ten minutes and closed the door on them. She put the plunger away, changed clothes, and picked up a few things. She finally let them in, and apologized. They looked around for a little while and left. After they left, she thought, if they buy the house, it has to be God. Yep, you guessed it; they put a bid on the house and ended up buying it. The closing on the house was set for the last week of June 2008.

Connie looked online for houses for rent in the Ellwood City area; she also talked with her family about helping us find a place to rent. After a couple of weeks of searching, she found a house close to her family that was in our price range. Connie's parents went and looked at the house for us; they also took some photos and emailed them to us. We liked the photos and what her parents said about the house, so we signed a year lease. The next thing we had to do was look into a truck to move with. I did all the research on that. We decided to go with U-Pack; it is a twenty-four-foot trailer that the company drops in your driveway and you load it. They pick it up and deliver it to where you are moving.

Connie once again enlisted the help of her parents and also got Mark to come help with this move. (I was getting very tired of moving.) I could not thank them enough for all their help—what a blessing they were. As we packed up the house, we put a lot of the boxes in the garage, so when we loaded the trailer, they would be easily accessible.

I started to look for jobs in the area where we would move. The place I worked had a job network that I could watch and see if any jobs opened up. There were a couple that did, I applied for them all, interviewed, and did not get any of them. I would have taken any position they had just so I had a job to go to. We kept praying, as we knew it would work out. God has always been faithful to us, and He would provide a job.

Everything was falling into place. We knew that this was the right choice for us; God was working it all out. There were no problems with any paperwork, the buyer's financing was approved, and the closing was set for June 28. We did not have to be present for the closing; we signed a power of attorney so the realtor could sign the paperwork for us.

Mark and his parents arrived at our house on June 26. We would load the trailer the next day and leave Chicago the day after. Mark, his dad, and I did most of the loading of the trailer. Connie and her mom finished the packing and cleaning the house. What a job it was to pack the trailer! It took us the best part of the day to load it. Where does one collect so much? We had cleaned out the closets, gone through almost everything we had, and gotten rid of a lot of items. Even having done that, we still had lots of stuff. We used a lot of the trailer. When we had everything packed, we put up the dividing wall that the trucking company provided; they would load the remaining space with other freight.

We spent the night in the empty house. Connie and I slept on our mattress on the floor. Mark slept in one bedroom on an air mattress, as did Connie's parents in the other bedroom. I still did not have a job to go to. The district manager from Chicago contacted the district manager in Pennsylvania, explained our situation to him, and asked if he could help find a position for me. He replied that there were two places that might call me with a position, so we had to wait and see how this would all play out. We still believed God would work it out for us. We got up early and loaded the things that were left, got on the road, and headed to Pennsylvania.

Mark drove his truck, Connie's dad drove our little car, and Connie and I drove our truck. The trip went very well. We drove into a bad thunderstorm for a while and had to slow down for that. A little while later, it passed and we were able to resume the speed limit. We made good time and arrived at Connie's parents about a half hour before our appointment with the real estate agent to look at the house and sign the lease. Connie already had the utilities set to be activated on July 1.

We met the real estate agent at the house. Our first impression of the house was good. It was a two-story brick house set back from the main road. The house sat on two acres of land. The landscaping was very nice with numerous mature trees: pine and apple. You could tell that someone at one time had put a lot of work into them. We liked what we saw and signed the lease.

It would be a few days before our trailer arrived, so we stayed at Connie's parents. We spent the time cleaning the house and relaxing before we moved in. We received the trailer on Friday evening; that way we once again had lots of help to unload our furniture.

For the first two weeks we were there, I did not receive any calls about possible jobs. I went to the locations in person and introduced myself to the human resources staff—with no response. I applied for an actual position at one location. When I went to the HR office, there was an individual with the HR person, making copies. When I introduced myself and explained what was going on, he spoke up with his back to me and said, "I was the one who interviewed you and we still do not have anything for you." I looked at the HR person, who was as stunned as I was by his response. I said thank you very much and left. Needless to say, I did not or would not work at that location. After about two weeks, I did receive a call from another location and was offered a position, which I gladly accepted.

This situation about the job was another way that God showed me that He had everything under control, that I would get a position but not in the location that I wanted, but where I would be needed. I am so thankful that God was in control; the people at the location were unbelievably supportive of us. Sometimes I think God looks down at me and has to chuckle, saying if only you would wait on me, you would not be so stressed at times. I have a lot to learn yet. Thanks, God.

Most of July was spent getting settled in our house and, for me, getting to know the area. Connie's family was a tremendous help to us in settling in. During that time, Connie had to find all new doctors because they were all in network with the major hospitals there. Not one of the major hospitals in Pittsburgh would take Aetna insurance, which is the insurance we had. Oh boy, the fun had just begun.

We had battled the last three times of cancer by ourselves. It would be strange to have others around to help us.

CHAPTER 24

Mark's House

IN 1999, CONNIE'S BROTHER Mark had bought an older house that needed some repairs. This was his first adventure in buying and fixing up a house. It was a two-story house on a hillside. The house had been built in the late 1800s and looked good for its age. Mark's goal was to do most of the work himself and pay for the repairs as he went along, so he would not have a house payment. As the work progressed, he found the house was in a lot worse shape than he thought. He had known some things would need rebuilding, but other things were a surprise. He had to rebuild the front porch and repair some of the foundation, replacing block work. He put a new roof on it as well. The house had a small addition on the back that had not been done well, so it needed to be ripped off and redone. When Connie and I moved back to Pennsylvania in July 2008, he had been working on the house for about nine years, with help from a few friends and some relatives.

In late July, Connie and I started to help him on his endeavor. We would go out on Saturdays or after I got home from work. I would arrive home from work around 3:30 p.m. and be in the house for a few minutes before Connie would ask me, "What are you going to do tonight?" At first I would tell her if I needed to cut grass or do some chores around the house, and then I finally figured out what she wanted to do. "Let's go out and help Mark on the house." I always agreed to go, as I enjoyed doing that anyway, plus it was time spent with family and creating memories.

It got to the point with Connie that I would come home from work and would see snack bars, water bottles, and, of course, her insulated coffee mug sitting on the counter. I would say, "I see we are going to Mark's to work on the house, huh?" She would answer, "Yes, I told him we would be out as soon as you got home." I would chuckle to myself, go change clothes, and we would leave. Sometimes I would be tired and not want to go, but I knew she was home all day and needed to get out of the house, plus, as you know already, she loved to do projects.

We only got to help from July to late October before it got too cold. The following is what we accomplished: We put a second story on the addition, which was a major feat. Before we moved to Pennsylvania, Mark had the first floor of the addition completed; it was eight feet wide by the length of the house. He was going to put a bathroom and a sunroom down there. The second floor had to have the back half of the roof taken off the house and the top part of the new addition walls up so we could build the roof trusses to attach to the new addition from the center of the roof. We knew it was late in the year to do roof work, but we went for it. After we cut the first hole in the roof, there was no turning back. We could tell Mark was not too sure about cutting the hole in the roof, but he did it anyway. Looking back, we wondered what in the world were we thinking? Beginning so late in the year, knowing we had to have it done by the time the snow started to fly.

We did a section at a time, about five to six feet, and covered the space with tarps until we could resume the work. At some point, we would need a break, so most of the time someone would make the trip into Ellwood City to a local fast-food restaurant and order two large black coffees and an iced tea. At the time, one had a promotion of two mini pumpkin pies for a dollar, so we would enjoy our treats and get back to work. Sometimes on our way to Mark's house, we would stop and pick up the usual and save a trip. At the time, it did not seem like much, but it was building memories that we talk about even now. I do not know how many trips we made to the big-box home improvement store to get two-by-fours, OSB sheeting for the floors or roof, and boxes of nails for the nail guns. We put down OSB on all the floors in the house. Connie and I would cut the boards and Mark would nail them down. Connie loved power tools, especially air nail guns. Mark let her use the nail gun as much as she could handle. The smaller nails she had no problem with; it was the larger ones she could not handle much. When you pull the trigger with the bigger nails, you get more kickback than you do with the little nails. Mark or I would help her hold the nail gun down, so she could use it.

We put up all the walls in the house, some windows, and a few doors. Most of the time spent was on the second-story addition and the roof. We put on the last piece of OSB late one evening as it was snowing a little bit and cold. Connie was bundled in my heavy work coat plus the others layers of clothing she had on. She tried to help us, but she got cold easily. She did not stray too far from the propane heater Mark had to give us some heat. She would wander away for a bit to hand us tools or clean up. We nailed the last nail, put the ladders away, and went home for the winter.

We accomplished a lot in the few months we worked on the house that year.

In the spring of 2009, we did not help on the house much; we only went out a handful of times. Connie was losing weight and not doing well, though she was able to hide it. The few times we did go out and help, we only stayed for a couple of hours. She was in a lot more pain and could only handle so much.

The last time Connie was out at the house, Mark and I were removing the asphalt-type siding from the house. We removed as much as we could by using smaller ladders and leaning out windows. It was at the point that we had to go up high on the ladders when Mark said he would go up the ladder if I would stay below and keep the ladder steady. Connie was sitting on a lawn chair and saw Mark going up the ladder. When she saw how high he was going up and what we were doing, she got upset and asked where the safety harness was that Mark bought when he put the shingles on the roof. The roof was very steep, so he had purchased it for that reason. After Connie and Mark went back and forth for a while, we got the safety harness out and secured it so Mark was able to remove the rest of the siding.

CHAPTER 25

The Courage to Be Imperfect, Part Two

IN AUGUST 2008, SOME of Connie's family went to see the progress being made at Mark's house. I do not remember who all was there; I was not because I was at work. On the way home, they discovered a coffee shop they had not seen before in a little strip mall. The name of it was Thanks a Latte. They met the owners, Rick and Karen, who were working at the counter. Everyone enjoyed the coffee; at some point later in the day, they told the rest of us about this new place.

All Connie needed to hear was coffee shop; she loved a good cup. As for me, I never acquired a taste for it. I can tell you that over the years Connie tried everything she could to get me to drink coffee. I like the smell of it, but I do not like the taste.

Thanks a Latte soon became a hangout for us; we got to know Rick and Karen quite well. It was not a huge place. When you walked in the door, you were in the sitting area to the left with six to eight tables and chairs. There was another room to the left about the same size as the main room with a fireplace, sofa, tables, and a small bar. The first table on the left was called the family table, where Rick and Karen sat when they had no customers. We got to know them well enough that, whenever we came in, we had to sit at the family table.

On one of our visits, there was a book signing going on for a local person who had written a book about the area during the Victorian era. In the back room, during our conversation, Connie told them she and Mark had written a book about Connie's life. Karen took off and ran with that. She said they needed to do a book signing for her. This was a dream of ours to have book signings and speaking engagements to help people going through cancer. Just think, here in Ellwood City, Connie would have her first book signing! We arranged to come back at a later date to work out the details.

On our next visit to the coffee shop, Connie and Karen worked out the details of the book signing. It would be on November 22 from 1:00 to 5:00 p.m. Karen would take care of the publicity; they knew a reporter at the local newspaper. She would set up an interview for Connie with the reporter, and the interview would take place on November 18. We found out from the reporter, whose name was Louise, that she wanted to have Mark there as well in order to get his thoughts.

The day of the interview, I had to work. I really wanted to go, but oh well, one has to work. When I arrived home, Connie was waiting for me. She had so much to tell me and was very excited. The interview had gone really well. Louise had brought a photographer along to get some photos, which surprised everyone. Connie gave me all the details on the questions she asked and what was said. We now had to wait for the article to run in the paper. (You can still read the interview online at www. ellwoodcityledger.com; do a search on Connie Sabo and the article will come up.)

I was so proud of Connie. Part of her dream was about to come true. Her main desire was getting her story out and helping people going through cancer. We started to get ready for the book signing. Connie wanted to pass out flyers at the local churches and stores. We made the flyers and then Connie and Nancy went out one afternoon to pass out flyers and hang them wherever they could. We also had to order books to sell at the book signing. We were as ready as we could be for the event to take place. Both of us were very excited and in anticipation of how the book signing would turn out; all we could do now was wait.

November 22 arrived soon enough. We loaded everything in the car and headed to Thanks a Latte. When we arrived, Karen had three tables set up in the back room for us. One was for Connie, one for me (I was selling the books), and the other one was for Mark. People started to arrive at 1:00 p.m. At first it was a lot of Connie's family and relatives, and then others. The guests would come to me first and purchase a book, then go to Connie and Mark to have their book signed if they chose to do so.

It was so much fun, getting to meet new people and talk to them. It is amazing how many people are touched or affected by cancer. It was also nice to meet people I had heard about from different family members but hadn't met. It was nice to put a face to the name. I watched Connie a lot; she was in her element. She could walk into a room filled with people and, before she left, she would have met everyone. It was also very nice to see everyone drinking coffee and hanging out; some people stayed for a while and others just for a little bit.

Connie got to share her story with a lot of people that day, encouraging people and offering hope that cancer can be overcome. Before we knew it, 5:00 p.m. was here and it was time to pack up the books and leave. We went out for dinner and celebrated that evening. This was such a milestone we had achieved, so it needed to be celebrated, and that we did. We could not thank Rick and Karen enough for allowing us to have the book signing at their shop. We were so grateful to them for helping one of our dreams come true.

As a result of the book signing, the local Rotary Club invited Connie to come and speak at one of their upcoming meetings. After a few phone calls with one of the Rotary members, a date was set for the middle of

January 2009. Wow, a book signing and now a speaking engagement. We were sure that this would be the start of what Connie and I wanted to do. A verse in the Bible states, "Do not despise the days of small beginnings..."(Zechariah 4:10;NLT [New Living Translation]). It all has to start somewhere and we knew that Connie's hometown would be the starting point.

We figured Connie had about twenty minutes for her talk. She spent a lot of time putting the talk together. She made an outline and edited it a few times. Every time she edited it, I listened and timed her, so she could get it within the allotted time. We had fun with that. When you really listen to someone, you hear the littlest things. One thing she said frequently was um. When she tried not to say um as much, it was a lot harder to do when she consciously tried to correct saying it. After a few more tweaks, she was ready.

A few days before Connie was to speak, we received a phone call at 2:00 a.m. Connie answered the phone and it was Cindy, who had been a very, very close friend to Connie and me for years. Her daughter Nicole had been taken to the hospital and was not doing well. Let me give a few more details on what led up to this point.

Nicole is the daughter of J and Cindy. She was their only child. She was twenty-five years old and was married. She had one child named Elijah and was pregnant with their second child. Nicole was expecting the arrival of their child in January 2009. The doctor put her on bed rest prior to this. J and Cindy went to her house and helped with preparing meals and getting things ready for when she would come home after the delivery. Their child arrived right on time. Alyssa was born on January 1 and was the New Year's baby for that hospital. Mother and daughter were doing fine and were soon to go home.

When we received the phone call, we started to pray. We prayed throughout the night. Cindy would call and give updates. The updates were not very good, but we kept praying. I had to go to work; Connie was to call me and give me updates as she received them. About 9:00 a.m., Nicole passed away. It was a shock to everyone. J and Cindy were devastated. The doctors had no answers as to what had happened. They would have to wait for the post mortem findings. I cannot go into detail as to what the cause was due to privacy issues.

This rocked all of us and Connie had a hard time with it. I went to my work management, explained the situation, and they let me go home. Connie and I decided that we needed to go to North Carolina and be with J and Cindy. We wanted to go now and help them in any way we could before their families started to arrive. I arranged for a few days off and we left the next morning. J and Cindy said that we did not need to come down because Connie was not feeling well at times. We did not tell them we were coming down until we were on the road for a few hours; that way, they could not argue with us.

We arrived in Asheville and checked into our hotel. J and Cindy came by for a little while. I know they were very happy that we were there. The next couple of days we helped them, supported them, and let them talk. We knew we had to go back to Pennsylvania, although we did not want to. I had to go back to work and a lot of their family was scheduled to arrive from out of state. It was so hard to say goodbye, knowing what they were going through.

We got in the car and headed north. We usually stopped about every two hours to change drivers; we had found that this helped both of us not to be so tired when we arrived at our destination. On this trip, Connie did not want to drive; that was unusual for her because she loved to drive. She was not feeling well and the trip was wearing her down.

After being home for a couple of weeks, Connie received the call from the Rotary and a new date was set, it would be the first part of March. Sometimes time flies; here we were on our way to the meeting. The meeting was held in the clubhouse at the local golf course. We arrived to find there was a buffet dinner first. The food was very good. They sat us at the head table with the president and the other officials of the organization. After dinner, they attended to their business, and then Connie finished up the meeting with her story. Connie did an awesome job; she held to her twenty minutes. Most people who hear her story are amazed by her. We also brought some books to sell that evening. Connie also signed and donated a copy of her book to the local library.

When we arrived home, we talked a lot about the evening. I was so proud of her and it was a very happy time—something good amidst the ongoing saga of cancer and all the doctors' appointments.

I discovered later that I had part of the speech Connie made for the Rotary. I am including it here for your pleasure:

> Hello! I am Connie Sabo. I'm here to talk to you a little about my book, *The Courage to Be Imperfect*. The book is a collection of my memoirs and contains what I felt to be some of the events leading to the development of what I was told was a rare and unusual mindset. At the time the book was published, I had survived four episodes of cancer, the first one at the age of seventeen. The following three episodes over the next thirty-plus years were breast cancer. I was raised in Ellwood City, in North Sewickley Township. I had a reasonably average childhood. I attended Riverside High School and, depending on who you ask, was an above-average student. I went with my parents to Providence Baptist Church for many years and received a solid foundation Biblical teaching and doctrine. Between there and home, a strong sense of values began to develop.
>
> Like I said, the first episode of cancer came about the end of my senior year. This was difficult for all involved because "kids aren't supposed to get cancer." I developed

a bit of a tough-guy attitude but was hurting inside. This effort to take the emotional burden off others cost me a lot of years of pain until I worked through all that. The greatest healing time up to that point was in my early thirties and involved a return to my Christian faith and beliefs. I can take very little credit for the healing except for having the guts to move through it. After all, pain is usually a temporary state.

CHAPTER 26

Spots on the Liver

ONE OF THE BLESSINGS of moving back to Pennsylvania was that Connie's family was there. They helped us out so much in taking Connie to her doctor's appointments. Usually, it was Connie's mom and dad, or if Mark was off work, he took her. I was used to going to Connie's appointments with her. When they took her, I didn't get to be there when the doctors talked to her and get that firsthand information.

This was bittersweet. When I got home from work, after getting settled in for a few minutes, I would always ask her how her doctor's visit went. Connie told me the gist and what the doctor had said. Sometimes she was not forthcoming with a lot of information. Sometimes I would have to ask a lot of questions to get some of the answers. I think sometimes that she had plenty of time after being home from the appointment to process all the information and figure out how to edit what she'd tell me.

One particular doctor's appointment was a regular follow-up visit and also to get the results of the previous PET scan. The time frame for this was around the end of June 2009. I think sometimes that when you've been through seeing so many doctors and having numerous scans, you can become complacent, like you've heard it all before. You've heard its cancer, the cancer has spread, the scans look good, you are doing great, and on and on.

All it takes is one question as to how an appointment went with an answer of certain results to shock you back into reality.

I arrived home from work and did the usual things you do when you get home from work. Connie was in the study, and when I walked in, I looked at her. I could tell something was different. I leaned down and kissed her because she was sitting on the couch. I sat in the office chair and we started to talk. Then I asked the question: "How was the meeting with the doctor?" Connie's reply was something I had never heard before: "We'll talk about that in a little bit." I was not used to that because she would usually give me the highlights.

I didn't like the way this sounded, but I took a deep breath and figured she would talk about it when she was ready. About a half hour later, Connie was ready to talk about the visit. Connie was not one for beating around the bush, as you know from reading this book. She was blunt about it. She said they got the results of the PET scan today and there were spots on her liver that were cancerous.

Nothing we had been through hit me like this did. Spots on the liver— those words truly took my breath away. I knew from dealing with this cancer and from other experiences that spots on her liver were not good. Normally, I could keep good composure and deal with whatever the news was at a later time. This time, I couldn't. I tried to choke back the tears. I got quiet, but I couldn't choke back the tears anymore. I tried, I really tried to suck it up, but it didn't work.

I knew from all these appointments that we were dealing with stage IV cancer, but there was always hope. This, spots on the liver, needed a miracle from God. I was so desperately trying to choke back tears, but I finally blurted out, "I'm sorry for the tears." Connie replied, "It's okay. I had my share of them before you got home." She said she was happy that she'd had the time by herself until I arrived home, so she could wrap her head around all of it. At this point, she also started to cry, which broke my heart even more.

I didn't know what to say. I couldn't talk about what I wanted to. I wasn't wailing in my tears, I wasn't out of control, it was just sobs. This was the first time I had cried in front of her during the entire cancer saga. I had my share of private times when I cried, but not in front of her because I wanted to be strong for her. I don't know that I can describe the wave of emotions that hit me all at once. I had not been expecting this.

Finally, Connie said that there were approximately five spots on her liver. She said one thing they could do was to go in microscopically and put what she called little chemo balls on the cancer spots. That was the kind of treatment they could do for this. Regular chemo was not an option. We had some time to think about what we wanted to do. This decision did not have to be made right then and there.

We never had to decide anything about this because the decision was made for us.

CHAPTER 27

Time in the Hospital

IN THE LAST WEEK of June 2009 (I don't recall what day it was), I came home from work to see my in-laws' car in the driveway. That was not unusual because they would stop by to see Connie or she would invite them over for coffee or have them take her to a doctor's appointment. I didn't think Connie had an appointment that day, so I assumed they were there visiting.

I went into the house, saw my mother-in-law in the kitchen, and knew something was wrong. Ramona said, "Connie's on the couch and you need to go talk to her." Okay, I replied and went to the living room. Connie's dad was sitting on the love seat across from Connie, who was lying on the couch. I looked at her and she looked at me. I knew something was up. I walked over, gave her a kiss, and asked what was going on. Connie replied that she was not feeling well, that she had gotten really weak and couldn't get off the couch, so she had called her mom and dad and asked them to come over. Connie said she hadn't eaten much and thought her blood sugar was very low, so her mom got her some juice. She felt better but had still called the doctor and told him what was happening. The doctor said he wanted her to go to the hospital.

I just stared at her for a moment, thinking, now what? I think Connie saw that because she said, "We need to go the hospital. Can you go upstairs and pack an overnight bag?" I was shocked and didn't know what to say besides okay. I went upstairs and packed her overnight bag. Connie's mom got an insulated mug from the kitchen and put some juice in it for Connie to take with her. I finished packing her bag and went downstairs and said, "Okay, I'm ready."

It had been over an hour since Connie's mom and dad had come over and got some juice in her. We helped Connie get off the couch and walked her to the car. I tossed her overnight bag in the trunk and off we went to Butler Hospital once again.

I knew when we started down the road that this was going to be a long night. The ride from the house to the hospital was approximately 45 minutes, so we had a chance to talk all the way there. Connie continued to drink juice and by time we got to the hospital, she was feeling pretty good. I pulled up to the admitting area, retrieved a wheelchair, and helped her in. She sat outside the door until I went and parked the car. She was not ready to go inside just yet. I arrived back at the admitting door and wheeled Connie into admitting. We did all the paperwork needed to get her registered, which took about an hour, and then someone arrived and escorted Connie up to her room. By this time, it was 5:00 or 6:00 p.m.

We didn't realize that, by time we got checked in, it would be during the nurses' shift change. If we would have thought about that, we would have waited at the house a little bit longer before heading to the hospital. But here we were and now the wait was on for the shift change and the new nurse asking the million and one questions. They started Connie on an IV—so what else is new? They then hooked her up to the monitors, which had been the normal routine for every trip we made to the hospital over the years.

A few weeks before this episode of life with Connie, she was losing a lot of weight and not eating well. She had a hard time keeping food down. The doctors decided to put a feeding tube in, to help Connie get more nutrition and help her gain more weight. I was going to do a whole chapter on this, but I decided not to, the name of the chapter was going to be "The Feeding Tube from Hell." From the first day the feeding tube was put in, Connie experienced significant pain in the area where it entered her stomach. The doctor stated that it would take a little time for her body to get used to the tube being there.

Connie and I talked about this. Her view was that it would help her. She seemed to be okay with it; she thought it would be a temporary thing. I could tell that she was mixing a lot of faith with the power of the spoken word. As for me, I was not happy with it, but if it would help her put on weight, so be it. I knew I had to agree with her in faith.

"Truly I tell you, whatever you bind on earth will be bound in heaven, and whatever you loose on earth will be loosed in heaven.

"Again, truly I tell you that if two of you on earth agree about anything they ask for, it will be done for them by my Father in heaven. For where two or three gather in my name, there am I with them" (Matthew 18:19–20; New International Version [NIV]).

No matter who examined her, no one could tell her why the site hurt. One idea proposed was that a nerve was cut during the operation. The night we came home after the feeding tube was placed, the home healthcare nurse came to show us how to use it. Her first comment was "Why is the tube so long?" It was over three feet long. "And why did he place it there?" This was the first comment of all the healthcare personnel. One doctor said, "What the hell was he thinking? I've never seen this before!" The other doctor in his group made the same comment.

A week or two into the hospital stay, I arrived at my usual time at Connie's room. I walked into the room. Connie was sitting up in bed with her arms wrapped around her knees. In front of her legs toward the foot of the bed was a pile of vomit. She was crying; she never cried so I knew there was a problem. She looked up at me and said, "Please help me! I have been hurting so badly and have been pushing the help button for forty-five minutes and no one will respond."

I spun around and went out the door into the hallway and said in a really loud voice, "I need some help in here! Now!" Within thirty seconds, there were nurses everywhere; it took them less than fifteen minutes to get Connie cleaned up. The nurse administered some pain medication and soon Connie dozed off to sleep. I was absolutely furious! I understand how busy nurses are, as I am married to one. Connie only asked for help when she needed it. And forty-five minutes was way too long to respond. I reported this to the appropriate person.

Finally, everyone left, Connie was asleep, and I sat in my customary chair watching her. I was able to start to process what had happened. I'm a person who does not and will not allow myself to lose my temper. I got upset and angry this day when I saw Connie curled up in a ball and the look on her face. You know from before that her pain tolerance was extremely high, so for her to get to the level of pain she had was totally unacceptable. I talked and prayed to God for a while to get to the point where I could handle this. As I write this, God once again amazes me. He let me complain and gripe to Him, and even allowed me to be upset with Him. Through all that He still loved me. He wrapped his arms around the both of us. He loved us at that time when I couldn't see it, but now I can. I am so grateful to Him for holding us and loving us.

There were nurses in and out of Connie's room all night. The nurse assigned to Connie that night was a very young nurse in her mid-twenties. She took amazing care of Connie all that night. Connie awoke at one point, looked at me, and said "Please don't leave me tonight. I need you here!" I replied, "I won't." When she drifted off to sleep, I stepped out of the room, called work, and told them I would not be in the next day.

The next morning, Connie was feeling a lot better. Once they got breakfast and the change of shift out of the way, Connie and I talked for a long time. The result of the conversation was that she wanted the feeding tube removed. She could not handle the pain. We spoke to the doctor when he came in and he said he would have it removed. I had mixed emotions about the removal of the feeding tube. I knew Connie was receiving nourishment through it, but after last night and the pain she went through I had to be okay with it being gone. I think it was the next day that the doctor who installed the feeding tube came in and took the feeding tube out. I had to leave the room when that happened. It took about ten minutes. Within the next few hours, Connie was a different person and I could not believe the difference in her.

To understand fully this next episode of life with Connie, you need to read Chapter 2, "Changes," in her book. Sometimes I wish I could remember the names of certain nurses that entered our lives and our stay in the hospital, but I can't. This particular nurse was excellent with the care she gave to her patients. This day had to be on a weekend because I remember her in and out of the room all day. Connie was not feeling well all day, just a rough day for her. It was midafternoon when her nurse came in and did her usual duties of checking her vital signs and such. She started to walk out of the room but turned around and came back to Connie's bed, saying she had an idea. Sometimes I make a chocolate shake for some of the patients. I make it out of yogurt and I want to make one for you, as I know it'll make you feel better!

I looked at Connie. Her jaw dropped and she was speechless. I knew what she was thinking because I was thinking the same thing. When Connie was sixteen years old, over thirty-four years ago, the nurse said, "I'll be right back". She returned with a chocolate shake she made for Connie. When the nurse left the room to make the chocolate shake, Connie lit up like a Christmas tree. "Gabe, Can you believe that? She is making me a shake! I can't believe it, what are the chances of that? Write this down, we need to remember this so I can write about in my next book."

The nurse came in and handed Connie a chocolate shake. It was not very large, but the smile on Connie's face was priceless. As I write this years later on my back deck in the sunshine, I travel back in my mind and replay the scene over and over again. What this nurse did for Connie was such a small thing, but for Connie it was the best medication anyone could have given her. She talked about it for days.

I don't think there are coincidences in life; I think they are God moments—our Divine appointments. God has our lives planned out every day, every moment. He did this just for Connie. He created the second shake to help her get through the rough times she was having. Look at how much He loved her. He loves you the same way. Take the time to stop and smell the roses and you will see the God moments in your life if you look.

Connie was in the hospital the whole month of July 2009. She did not have a private room at first. There were multiple people who were there sharing the room with her at different times. Most of her roommates were not there very long, maybe a few days at a time. There were times they did not give her a roommate, which was nice so we could be alone. Connie had the bed by the door, so all the visitors for the other patients had to walk past us.

Connie usually made friends with the other patients who were in the room with her. During the day, there were not a lot of visitors, so she got to know most of them. One day she got a new roommate, an older woman in her late fifties or early sixties. I remember when she arrived because I think it was the whole family, six to eight people with her. It was a circus. They were very loud, not too courteous for being in a hospital room. Ruby was having breathing issues. She was not feeling good and her kids did not help her much. They kept asking for money to go get food and a drink. The TV was on and kind of loud. Then the kids would argue with Ruby. When Ruby's family was there, Connie did not get much rest.

After the first night with the whole clan in the room, we were exhausted. The kids were in and out, loud arguing, total commotion.

Connie and I talked about it. Out of all our hospital stays, this had to be the worst roommate ever. I had to work every weekday and I had almost an hour drive home, so I left about 9:30 or 10:00 p.m. But Connie could not leave; I would usually call her before I went to bed to check on her and most nights the family was still there.

During the day, Ruby would get phone call after phone call from her kids. Most of the time, the call would end in an argument. During the third or fourth day of Ruby's stay, Connie got to know her a little bit. Connie could get anyone to talk. Ruby had a rough life with a lot of issues. Connie told Ruby her story and that she had written a book about it. Connie called me, asked me to bring one of her books, and she gave it to Ruby.

One day Connie was not feeling well. During the afternoon, Ruby told Connie that she knew she was not feeling well but asked if she could wash Connie's hair for her. She told Connie it helped her and made her feel better. Connie gladly accepted this and let Ruby wash her hair and it did make her feel better.

Connie told me about it when I arrived at the hospital later that afternoon. She was so happy that someone else thought of this and had taken the time to do it. Most people won't take the time to do the simple acts of kindness. Ruby was discharged from the hospital a day or two later. Connie was sad to see her go, but that is the way it goes.

A week or two later, fluid was building up around Connie's heart. The doctors needed to drain it and they also wanted install a PICC (peripherally inserted central catheter) line, which is a port on the skin that connects to a main artery. It is an access point for the nurses to give shots and put in IVs. To insert the PICC line, they had to put Connie under sedation. They scheduled the surgery and when she came out, they put her in intensive care, so she could be closely monitored since her heart started to race again. Everything turned out fine as far as the PICC line went, but she had to be in intensive care until they could get her heart rate back down. She was feeling okay but slept a lot.

One evening, Connie had a visitor and it was Ruby. She had come back to the hospital to see Connie. She tracked her down in ICU. Connie was awake when Ruby arrived. Ruby started to chatter about all kind of things. She told Connie how she was doing and what was going on with her. Then she asked about Connie. Connie and I gave her an update on why she was in ICU. Ruby was truly concerned about Connie. Ruby was about ready to leave and asked if Connie needed anything. Connie replied that no, she was fine. Ruby said, "Connie, if you need anything at all, you let me know, and if you are hungry, I will go by McDonalds and get you a Big Mac." Connie graciously said no thank you and Ruby left. Connie and I looked at each other and said, "Big Mac?"

Connie was in ICU and could not eat much. It was the innocence of Ruby and the sincerity of Ruby. She would have gone and gotten a Big Mac for Connie if she wanted it. We chuckled about it for a few days. It was a moment in life that we needed to take our minds off all the medical issues we were going through. We never saw Ruby again.

CHAPTER 28

The Doctor from Hell

CONNIE WAS DOING BETTER and really seemed to be improving. She was eating better, the feeding tube was out, and she also looked good. One day, I arrived at the hospital after work at 4:00 p.m. When I walked in the room, she was sitting up in bed and seemed different. She had eaten well that day. I kissed her, pulled up a chair alongside the bed, and we talked. She asked about my day. We talked about her day in the hospital. Not much had gone on; that was a good day for her.

We sat and talked for quite a while. The hospital staff came in with Connie's dinner. She started to eat, so I went down to the cafeteria to get some food for me. I brought my meal back up to her room and ate with her. She ate a good bit of hers. It was really good to see that she was hungry. I can tell you, that made me very happy.

Not long after we finished eating, Mark came in. Connie was clearly very happy to see him. He handed her a magazine, saying that he had gotten it for her. The magazine was about island paradises. He told her that when she got out of the hospital, she could pick the island and we would go. Once Connie saw that, it was game on. All of us love the beach and the tropics. It was Mark's way of brightening up her day. We all sat and talked for a while about where we would want to go and what we would want to do. Usually, for Connie and Mark that consisted of reading a book on the beach, and for me picking up seashells. We laughed, we joked around, and it was a really good evening.

I watched Connie and Mark interact. It was so good to see Connie in really good spirits. When I was there with Connie by myself, I usually pulled up a chair alongside the bed close to her so we could talk. But when someone arrived, like Mark that particular evening, I pushed my chair back against the wall at the foot of the bed so we were sitting side by side facing Connie. There we were, having a good time.

At 7:00 or 7:30 p.m., a doctor we had never seen before entered the room, or rather he did not come all the way into the room, but stood partly in the hallway. "Mrs. Sabo?" he inquired.

Connie replied yes.

The doctor, looking at Mark and me, asked, "Who are these two?"

"This is my husband, Gabe, and my brother, Mark," said Connie.

"Okay, so you're all family?"

Connie said yes. At that point, we looked at each other, wondering who this guy was and what he wanted. We were about to find out.

"I am Dr. So-and-So." (I don't recall his name nor do I ever want to.) "I need to tell you that we received the results back from the test of the fluid that is in your chest. The fluid has cancer cells in it. There's not a lot that can be done and it is not very good for you. You can talk to your regular doctor, but there's not a lot that he can do either. Do you have any questions for me?" After that, he left.

As he was talking to us, I was watching Connie. When he said there were cancer cells in the fluid, I saw an immediate change in Connie, though she held it together. I knew that totally rocked her world. I know I was speechless. I thought, dear God! What just happened? I looked over at Mark and his jaw was on the floor with a horrified look on his face. I looked back at Connie and I could tell she was not doing well at all. We all sat there in silence. I don't know how long that was, each one of us staring.

Finally, I said, "What in the world just happened?"

Nobody said anything. Connie looked at me, and with that look that I've seen quite a few times, said, "You guys need to go."

"What?" I replied

"You guys need to go home."

I was frozen in my seat; I didn't know what to do.

Mark got up and said, "I'm going to go. I'll see you later, Connie." I could tell Mark wasn't handling it well either.

As he left the room, Connie looked at me and said, "You need to go out with him." I said, "I want to be here." She said, "No, you need to leave, too."

I didn't know what to do. I wanted to stay, but she wanted me to go. I knew Connie well enough; she had been through so much that she needed to process this. I kissed her and left. I can tell you, it was a long walk to the car. My mind was reeling from what this doctor said. We had seen a lot of different doctors over the years, and this guy had the worst bedside manners of anybody I had ever seen in my life. We ended up reporting him to the hospital for his conduct. If it was Connie and I in the room by ourselves, that would be different, but Mark was there, and his doctor had no business saying what he said and how he said it with Mark in the room.

It was a long, long, long ride home. I was shell-shocked and numb. I didn't know what had happened, but I knew enough to understand that the information he gave us was not good. I prayed the whole way home, talking to God. I did not sleep well that night because my mind was reeling. I had a hard time going to work the next day; it was a very long day! I wanted to get back to the hospital and see Connie.

When I got there after work, the same nurse that Connie had the day before stopped me in the hallway before I arrived at Connie's room. She asked what had happened last night and what the doctor had said. I told

her and she was really upset about it. She said, "That is no way to do that."
She had also been there when Mark and I had left the night before. She
said that we were hardly out of the room before Connie was on the button
requesting a nurse. Connie was so shaken up by what the doctor had said
that she wanted something to put her to sleep, so the nurse gave her some
drugs to sleep.

I was relieved to hear that because all day I had wondered why she had
wanted me to leave. I knew that she needed time to deal with it. The nurse
said that Connie had told her the same thing that I had told her about the
doctor. She wanted to make sure of what was said because she was going
to report this doctor to the hospital.

In the room, I stood looking at Connie and noticed a total change in
her. She was so different from the night before. She was quiet and didn't
say a whole lot. We talked a little bit about what had happened the previous
night and what the doctor had said. Connie was still having a hard time
dealing with it and so was I. Connie kept asking for more pain medicine.
Usually, after receiving pain medication, she went to sleep. That particular
night, Connie was not awake much at all.

As I write this, I reflect back on that evening. It's like a video playing
in my brain. I know it's something that will take me a long time to forget.
I can't even imagine what was going on in Connie's head. I thought of
the mindset the doctor had previously confirmed where she could look
at things and see them as an obstacle to overcome. How did a person
overcome this? I see now why she wanted to sleep; she didn't want to have
to think about it. That night with the Doctor from Hell resulted in a major
shift in Connie. Mark and I talked later and he stated that once the doctor
said what he had to say, Mark looked at Connie and saw the wind go out
of her sails.

For me, it was another major foundation-shaking of my faith. I
questioned God. Why? What is going on? Again, the heavens were silent.
I've told a lot of people over the years that when I get to Heaven, I will

have a lot of questions to ask God. I had a revelation that once I get to Heaven, see all its beauty, and meet Jesus face-to-face, I won't care about the questions I've had nor will I need to ask them. In the Bible, it says there will be no tears in Heaven, no pain, no sickness or death or sin.

"And God will wipe away every tear from their eyes; there shall be no more death, nor sorrow, nor crying. There shall be no more pain, for the former things have passed away" (Revelation 21:4; New King James Version [NKJV]).

When we get there, we won't care what happened in this life because we achieve the ultimate prize, Heaven, and meet Jesus face-to-face.

CHAPTER 29

The Fall

IT WAS THE SECOND week of July 2009 and Connie was still in the hospital. She was doing okay and had two IV pumps going. I don't recall what all they were pumping, but there were at least four bags of IV fluids going simultaneously. Connie was in and out of consciousness, waking up to ask for more pain medication when needed. When she was coherent, I would take advantage of that and hold as much conversation with her as she was able.

She wasn't confined to the bed. She was still able to get up and go to the bathroom, but it required assistance because she had two IV pumps on different poles. It required quite an entourage for her to go to the bathroom. Before this, it had been no problem for her. The seat on the toilet had handles on each side for patients to use, which helped them get on and off the toilet. The handles are held in place by buttons you have to push in to unlock them. The button on the left side of Connie's toilet did not work, so the handle would slip out.

On one of the earlier trips to the bathroom, the nurse was helping Connie when the left handle came out as Connie went to sit on the toilet.

The nurse had to hold the handle for Connie to sit down and had to hold it again when she got up, so it would not come out. The nurse stated that they needed to fix that handle.

The next day, about midafternoon, the nurse was in doing her routine check. She looked at Connie and said, "How about if your husband takes you outside for a while? It's a beautiful day. We'll put you in a wheelchair and you guys can go sit for a while. It'll get you out of this room and let you get some fresh air."

Connie looked at her and said, "I can go outside?"

The nurse replied, "If you want to."

Connie said, "I would love to. Gabe, would you take me?"

"Of course," I answered.

The nurse said, "Okay then, let me go get a wheelchair and we'll get you hooked up and move the IV pumps to it, so you can be on your way."

I was shocked. I never thought about Connie being able to go outside. I don't know why that idea never occurred to me, but it didn't. I was excited and happy and I could tell Connie was happy, too.

The nurse left the room. Connie said she had to go to the bathroom, so I helped with the IV poles and pushed the poles as Connie went into the bathroom. I asked if she needed my help. She said she would be okay. She got into the bathroom; I pushed the IV poles in and closed the door. Ten seconds later, I heard a big crash and Connie screamed.

I pushed the door open and saw Connie sitting between the toilet and sink on the floor. I asked Connie is she was okay. No was her reply.

I grabbed the emergency button that was there in case you needed a nurse and pushed it. I knelt beside her. She looked up at me and it was one of the few times that I was able to see deep inside of Connie. I could see the pain, as she looked at me and said, "How much more do I have to take?" My heart broke once again. I didn't know how to reply.

The nurse came in and I told her that Connie had fallen. We got

Connie up and put her back in bed. The nurse examined her, asking where it hurt. Connie replied that it was her right side, her ribs.

I started to pray and asked God to help. I just stood there and watched. I couldn't believe this. I thought we were going outside, and now this? Before I knew it, there were three nurses in the room helping her. The first nurse asked Connie how she had fallen. Connie explained that when she went to sit down on the toilet, the handle had flown off. I went to the bathroom and looked at the handle that the nurse had held before. When Connie put pressure on it, it slid out and went into the shower. We did not think that when she went in by herself, someone had to hold that handle so it wouldn't slide out. We were thinking about getting her outside and forgot about the handle. Within ten minutes of Connie's statement about the handle coming off, there was a maintenance man there fixing the handle.

Her fall ruined the day for Connie going outside. They gave her pain medicine, which meant she would be sleeping shortly, but that was okay because she needed sleep and rest. A doctor came in, examined her, and said she should be okay, but he wanted to have X-rays done of her ribs to make sure nothing was broken or damaged. She had some scrapes on her sides and she was really sore, but I thank God, the X-rays came back and nothing was broken. She was in a lot of pain, though.

A few days later, Connie was feeling much better from the fall. I think it was a Saturday. The nurse asked her if she wanted to make another attempt to go out. Connie agreed, so the nurse and I started getting her ready. The nurse went to get a wheelchair and I helped Connie out of bed and positioned the IV poles so she could get into the wheelchair. We got Connie situated, and then we had the task of getting the IV pumps attached to the wheelchair. The nurse said that they could disconnect a couple of the IVs for the short time Connie would be gone. We only had to deal with one pump and two bags of IV fluids. The nurse took extra precautions; she put a couple of pillows by Connie's legs for cushioning.

We were ready to go and I pushed Connie out of her room and down the long hallway. We had to take an elevator to the ground floor and we went out the main exit. Connie was quiet as I pushed her outside, then she said, "Please put me in the sun." I put her in the sun out of the way from where others were gathered and locked the wheels on her chair. I sat on a bench next to her so we could talk.

The first thing Connie said was that it was so good to be sitting out in the sun again. This was something Connie had always enjoyed. We sat there for a little while, both of us quiet. "I have an idea," I said. "Let's take a photo of you with my phone and text it to Mark. For the photo, I need you to raise your hands like you are on a roller coaster. When we send the photo, we'll title it 'Escaping.'" She liked that idea and agreed Mark would enjoy it. We took the photo and sent it to Mark, both of us laughing, as we waited for his reply. Mark's reply was, of course, a snide comment I don't recall. It was nice to make a funny moment out of the process it took to get Connie outdoors.

We sat there for fifteen or twenty minutes. Connie asked me to push her to the other side, so she could see what was over there. The time between the first and second mastectomies we took up computer gaming. When we were ready to stop playing the game, Connie always had to see what was around the next corner. We stayed in the new spot for another 10 minutes, until she was ready to go in.

Back in her room, a couple of the nurses helped Connie get back in bed and, of course, they asked how her excursion was. We talked about that for a little bit. Before long, Connie dozed off. At the time, I don't think I saw how hard it was for Connie to make that trip. I realize now it took a lot of energy out of her, but I'm sure glad that we got to go outdoors and sit.

When Connie and I were by ourselves, we talked about her excursion. She really enjoyed it, but she didn't like being pushed through the main lobby to get there, with everybody staring at her. It was her perspective of being in the wheelchair or being pushed in the wheelchair. I did not pay attention to that, as I was happy we had been able to go outside.

CHAPTER 30

Lost, Dazed and Confused

I DON'T KNOW HOW to dive into this one, but here we go. It was Tuesday and I went to work. On my lunch hour, I would always call Connie and see how she was doing. After work on this day, I went to the hospital as I normally did. Connie and I had dinner together. About 6:00 p.m., Nancy and Brad arrived to visit Connie. One of the greatest things that happened that week was to see Connie's happiness at having Nancy and Brad there. She perked right up and her mindset also kicked in.

Nancy brought a cloth bag containing various scented lotions. She wanted to give Connie a massage. To see the look on Connie's face was so priceless. When people came to visit, they brought flowers or cards. When Nancy brought this for her, it made all the difference in the world. We all sat there and talked and Nancy started to massage her. Nancy did her legs, arms, and feet. Connie so enjoyed that. It was incredible to watch her, after the fall and all she'd been through.

While Nancy was rubbing in the lotion, Connie just chatted away. Nancy made a comment from a movie she loved called *Talladega Nights*. They started talking about the movie. Connie hadn't seen it. Nancy said they would just have to watch it. That started a whole other conversation between the two of them. Nancy said, "Let's do a girls' night this week." She would get in touch with Kylie, who is Nancy and Brad's daughter and they would come up. "When do you think, like Thursday night? We'll bring the laptop, the movie, and everything we need to give you a manicure. How about that?" Well, it was a date.

We decided that since Nancy would be there with Kylie, I could go home and catch up on a few things. I would run up to the hospital right after work on Thursday and leave after Kylie and Nancy got there that night. I was okay with that; it was time Connie and Nancy needed to spend together. Nancy and Brad left, and Connie and I talked about the evening and how happy and excited she was about Thursday night.

I went home about my normal time and went to work the next morning at 8:30. My phone rang. I saw by the caller ID that it was Connie. She never called unless it was important. "I'm not doing very well," she said. "You need to get to the hospital." I told her I was on my way. I didn't know what to think, I didn't know what was going on. I was shocked. I was working with one of my employees, Paula. I looked at her and said I had to go, that it was Connie. "Please tell management that I have to leave." The management knew that Connie was in the hospital and was aware of everything that was happening. There were a few times that I had to call into work and use the Family Medical Leave Act (FMLA) because I had to stay at the hospital.

It was a long trip to the hospital. I prayed and prayed and prayed all the way there. I had a lot of emotions going on inside me— uncertainty, anxiety, and not knowing what was going on. I had a lot of questions again for God—why? But there were no answers. I did not make phone calls to tell anybody because I didn't know what to tell until I got to the hospital to see why she called me. Then I would make the appropriate phone calls. It usually took close to an hour to get from work to the hospital, but this trip seemed like forever. I finally arrived at the hospital. I had to park in the parking garage and make my way to Connie's room.

When I arrived, a nurse was standing on her left side and Connie had a long tubular thing under her nose. Connie and I locked eyes, and it was another one of those moments that I could see deep within her that something wasn't right. I stood there and finally asked what was going on. "Everything went so well last night. She was good. What happened?"

The nurse told me they had to put this on Connie to help her get more oxygen. She wasn't getting enough oxygen with the regular device. This one holds more oxygen in reserve. I could tell the oxygen was turned up high as I could hear the rushing of the oxygen into the mask.

Connie did not talk much. I know now they had increased her dose of Dilantin, which kept her drowsy. By the time I arrived at the hospital, her doctors had already been there to examine her, so I did not get to talk to them about Connie and what was going on. Later that afternoon, they put in a catheter. Before that she would get up and use the bathroom on her own. Now they wanted her to stay in bed so she would not have an accident.

I did not like what was happening. I went out to the hallway, found her nurse, and asked what was going on. She said, "Gabe, you need to go in and shut the door and have a heart-to-heart with Connie. It is not good. You need to talk to her."

Back in the room, Connie was awake. I sat down and said we needed to talk about what is going on. She just stared at me for a minute or two and then pushed the button to call the nurse. The nurse came in and Connie asked for more Dilantin. Connie said, "Gabe, it'll be alright." The nurse came back and administered the Dilantin. Within a few minutes, Connie was back asleep.

I came to the realization that she could not cope with what was going on. I had to come to grips with how serious the situation was. I don't think she could handle leaving me. As you read in her book *The Courage to Be*

Imperfect that when she had the second mastectomy, I knew that all I could do was pray and that I did fervently. I know I begged God and pleaded with Him to heal her. I knew without a shadow of doubt that He could. I could not think about it much more, so I prayed.

Connie woke up at one point, looked at me, sat up, and said, "Give me a kiss." So I did. She lay back down and went to sleep. Later she woke up again, sat up, looked at me, and then took off her oxygen mask and tossed it at the foot of the bed. She just shook her head. I retrieved the mask and told Connie she needed to put it back on. She shook her head no and waved her hand and said no and just sat there. I asked her again, but she wanted no part of it. I pushed the button for the nurse who arrived within a minute or two and asked what was wrong. I told her Connie had tossed her oxygen mask and I couldn't get her to put it back on.

"Connie," the nurse said, "how are you doing? You know you need the oxygen." She picked up the oxygen mask and Connie allowed her to put it on. Go figure! I don't know what the difference was, but it worked. This happened three more times. Connie would wake up and go back to sleep. Her breathing started to get shallower and the time between her breaths got longer and longer. The nurse talked to me at one point and asked if Connie had any family. I replied that she did. The nurse said that I needed to call them in. This was a reality shock for me. In the back of my mind, I knew this was going to happen, but I wanted to stand firm in my faith, trusting God would heal her. She had beaten cancer four times. We could beat this again.

I prayed about this and wrestled with this in my head for a long time. What if I was wrong about calling Connie's family in? What if she would be okay? Then I thought what if I did not call the family in and she passed away? I would have to deal with that. Finally, about 1:00 a.m., as Connie's breathing started to get longer and longer between breaths, I called the family. This was one of the hardest choices I had to make, but I thought they had the right to be there, and if I were wrong, everyone would just lose sleep. I told the nurse that I had called the family and she replied that was a good choice.

The nurse made coffee and snacks in the waiting room down the hall for Connie's family. Each member of the family arrived at different times. When they arrived, I met them in the hall, explaining why I called. Everyone was very grateful. The room was semi dark and the rushing sound of oxygen was all you could hear. Connie's brother Rick noted that the way Connie was breathing was like a fish out of water trying to find oxygen.

Connie woke up, looked around the room, and saw all of her family there. I could tell that that freaked her out. Her family had never been there all at the same time. They had always come at separate times. She was used to seeing only a couple of family members and me in the room at the same time. Connie drifted back to sleep. It took a little bit, but I called everyone down the hall into the waiting room and explained what I had seen when she woke up. I thought it would be best for only a few of us to be in the room at one time. Everyone agreed. The next time Connie woke up and looked around, I could tell she was more at ease.

At 4:00 a.m., Nancy and I were the only ones in the room with Connie. When she woke up, she lay there for a moment, looking at me and then looking to her right, seeing Nancy. She sat up and pulled her legs up to her chest, wrapped her arms around her legs, and just sat there for moment. Then she looked at me and said, "It all has to do with Talladega Nights!" The look on my face must have been priceless. I looked at Nancy and she had the same look. I said, "Talladega Nights, huh?" Connie replied yep. I thought for a second and said, "Have you ever seen Talladega Nights?" Nope was Connie's reply, "but it all has to do with Talladega Nights." Okay, I said. She unwrapped her arms, lay back down, and drifted off to sleep.

Nancy and I looked at each other, got up, and left the room. Down the hall, we asked each other what that had been all about. We had no clue what she was referring to, but to Connie it made perfect sense.

To this day, I have no clue as to what she meant. Sometimes I think it was important, but then again maybe it was all the medication she was on. Three IV pumps plus what they were injecting into the port. Who knows? So much was running through my mind. I was trying to be strong in my faith and trusting in God that He would intervene. He could heal her and she would bounce back, but looking at the reality of the here and now, Connie could leave this world. I was tired and worn out emotionally and physically. God, please help me! My heart was aching seeing Connie like this. I pleaded with God, "Please don't take her. Take me instead. Her story, her life, You have brought her through so much. She could help so many people." I was totally serious with God. I would have taken her place. I now understand unconditional love.

The next morning, one of her doctors arrived, did her examination, and by looking at the chart and at the rate that Connie was asking for Dilantin decided to put Connie on a morphine drip to keep her comfortable. She pulled me aside and we talked. The gist of the conversation was that Connie had two days to live. She recommended that hospice be called in. I was not ready for this, even though in the back of my mind, I knew this was a possibility. She had pulled out of this type of situation so often; she could do it again. The doctor and I told the family, but no one wanted to hear that. Hospice would be there shortly and have a meeting with us to explain what they do and what to expect.

The doctor left the room and I excused myself from everyone. I needed to be by myself and process. The only thing I could think of was to go outside. I made my way out to the front of the hospital where I found a quiet place off to the side of the building. I was stunned and numb. Could this really be happening? Two days? I lost it and broke down. I had to pull myself together because if I didn't, I wouldn't be able to reel everything back in. I sat on the ground against the building and stared into space.

My next thought was to call Mom. I had to tell someone, so I dialed her number. "Hello? Hey, it's me. I just talked to the doctors and they said Connie has two days to live." Mom was quiet. I rattled on for a minute and then said, "Mom, I'm sorry." I knew there was nothing she could do, but I had to talk to someone. "Can you call Kathy and Rose and tell them for me? I don't think I have it in me." She replied, "Yes, I will."

I sat outside the hospital for quite some time trying to collect myself, still in disbelief. I took my time going back in. Upon arriving, I looked at all of Connie's family. They were not handling it any better. They told me hospice would be there in about an hour. Since there were people there, I asked the nurse if there was any place I could clean up. I desperately needed a shower. She made a phone call and then told me where to go. I gathered my belongings, my overnight bag, and headed down the long hallway. The whole time my mind was numb. I was like a zombie. Just point me in the direction I need to go.

It is amazing what a shower and clean clothes can do for you. I felt so much better. The lady from hospice arrived and we all went down to the waiting room, except for Connie's dad because he wanted to stay with her. We sat in a semicircle facing the hospice representative. As she started to talk, I looked around the circle. There was not a dry eye in the place. She went through the process of what happens. Everything she talked about Connie had gone through. The main priority was to make sure that there was enough medication to last through the weekend, and to help us in any way they could. The meeting lasted about a half hour and then she left.

Everyone was quiet. All of us sat there and we had to deal with what we had just heard. It was 1:00 p.m. by then. Everyone was exhausted and needed to go get some rest. It was the first time I asked for help from anyone. I asked if someone could help me through the night, that I didn't think I could make it. I was so tired. Nancy quickly spoke up that she and Brad would come and help me through the night. They needed to go home first and get some rest, and then they'd come back so I could get some rest. I was so grateful.

I made my way back to Connie's room. Her dad got up and left. I was alone with Connie once more. The sound of rushing oxygen on the gauge was maxed out at a ten. The sound of Connie trying to breathe prompted me to say, "God? Where are You? Please take me instead." I prayed and prayed and paced the room, praying. This went on for hours. If I sat too still, I started to fall asleep and I did not want that to happen. So I paced, praying, quoting every Bible verse I had memorized. The time was now 8:30 p.m. I was waiting for Nancy and Brad to arrive; I didn't know how much longer I could go on, as it had been over thirty hours of little sleep. I called Nancy to see what time they were arriving and she said they would arrive around 10:00 p.m. They did. I was so thankful for them being there to help me. Nancy said, "Go to bed and get some rest. If anything changes, I'll wake you."

I went to the bathroom, changed clothes, and then crawled into the extra bed in Connie's room.

I fell asleep, but any kind of unusual noise woke me up, as it had the previous night there. Every time I had heard Connie move or operate the bed, I had gotten up to help her. About an hour after I lay down, I got up to check on Connie and Nancy said go back to sleep. At 1:20 a.m., Nancy called, "Gabe! Gabe! Get up. Her breathing is changed." I shot out of bed. Connie was hardly breathing. I went over to Connie's bed on her right side and took her hand. Nancy was holding her other hand. Brad was at the foot of the bed.

I looked at her and said, "Connie go dance with Jesus, go dance your way across Heaven." A few seconds later, a tear came out of her right eye. Shortly after that, she took her last breath on this earth. Jesus was there and He was taking her home. The battle was over; she won. She's in Heaven and there's no more battle with that horrible word I despise, cancer. Over thirty years of warrior fighting. Now she's completely clean from the cancer.

I fell apart, finally able to let go—the pain of her not being there. But then I felt peace that she was in no more pain. I wept the longest time. At some point, I started to pray out loud; I don't recall the prayer. The nurse came back into the room to check vitals and shut off the oxygen. Finally! No more rushing sound of it pouring into Connie's mask. The nurse removed the mask and said. "Take as long as you need with her. There is no hurry."

I finally composed myself and looked at Nancy who was still weeping. A younger sister just lost her mentor, the person who helped raised her. There was a ten-year age difference between them. They had been so close. I could see Nancy's pain and that broke my heart even deeper. I looked at Brad who was not any better. He looked at me and said that he would call the rest of the family. I thanked him and he walked out to make the dreaded calls.

There was such a peace in the room I could tell it was a Heavenly peace. I was finally able to get off my knees from kneeling beside her bed. I stood at the foot of her bed and just stared at her. She was at rest, so peaceful. All I could do was to stand and stare at her. I was numb, broken, and exhausted, but yet I had to carry on. The caretaker mentality kicked in. The rest of the family would be there shortly and I had to get ready for them.

Brad came back into the room. Nancy was still sitting at Connie's side. The nurse came in and asked me what funeral home we wanted Connie to go to. I didn't know, having never thought of that. I looked at Brad who spoke up and said to call this particular one. Thanks, Brad! I was not prepared for that decision.

There was sadness in the room. Yet there was peace, comfort, no confusion, just peace. We all seemed to bask in that moment for a little bit. I told Nancy that, per Connie's wishes, there would not be a viewing. I told her if she wanted some time alone with Connie, we would leave the room. She said, "No, I had my time with her tonight."

I was not ready for the next thing that happened. Connie's parents arrived. We told them that Connie was gone. Connie's mom went to the side of her bed and kissed her daughter on the forehead. I fell apart once again. I did not think I had any more tears, but they kept flowing.

Rick and Amanda arrived next. To see the face of the younger brother seeing his sister lying there—more tears; my heart broke again. I wondered if I could make it through this, if my heart could make it. The next one was Mark. I didn't know if I could stand to see this, but I stood back and watched.

Mark stepped just inside the door and he could not see Connie. He looked at us when we told him she was gone. It was hard for me to watch. He walked farther into the room and saw his sister. I knew Mark well. He was broken, yet he tried not to show it.

God, please hold my heart, I don't think I can take anymore. I don't know what is holding it together; it must be Your hands.

About that time Pastor Andy, Connie's mom and dad's pastor walked in. Thank you, God! He started to console the family and I watched from a little distance.

After a little while, Pastor Andy spoke up and said let's all join hands and pray. That was what was needed at that point in time. It was so amazing and appropriate. After the prayer, I said, "Per Connie's wishes, there will not be a viewing. This is your viewing. If each of you want some time alone with Connie, we will be glad to leave the room." Pastor Andy said, "Gabe, there needs to be a viewing, so people can have closure." I quickly replied, "No! That is not Connie's wish." He tried to convince me, but I stood my ground. Everyone was okay with that decision. No one wanted private time with Connie, so we all just stayed for a little while longer and talked. It was now 3:30 a.m. and it was time to leave.

CHAPTER 31

Leaving

MOST OF CONNIE'S FAMILY said their goodbyes and left. Connie was in Heaven, although her body was still here. Mark and I watched each person say goodbye in their own way. Watching a father and mother leave their oldest child was something that they would not have dreamed of. Their child going to Heaven before them and the heartbreak of a brother and sister kissing their oldest sister goodbye, never to see her again. My heart was totally shattered.

The Bible says God collects all your tears. Mine that night were an ocean. I knew Mark and I had to leave at some point. As I looked around the room, I realized I had to clean out Connie's personal effects. I looked at Mark, who was in no better shape than I, and said, "I have to collect Connie's things." I got the blue duffle bag that I used to take Connie's things home and wash them and started to gather everything from the table beside her, the drawers, and the closet where she had extra clothes. What do I take and what do I leave there? The nurse gave us a hospital bag or two and Mark and I gathered what we could. I could not think. I told him to take what was important.

I asked Mark if he wanted time alone with Connie. He said no. He walked up to her, stared at her, touched her hair and then her cheek, leaned over and kissed her on the forehead. He stared some more and then left the room, saying he would be outside.

Now it was my time. I knew I had to keep this short. If not, I would not leave. I know I kissed her on the forehead and talked to her for a minute; I don't remember what I said. I was broken again, an ocean of tears. A man, totally broken to his core, his soul mate gone! The questions started to flood, now what? I fought the questions and thoughts. I knew I had to push on, like it or not. I stared at her one last time, kissed her forehead, told her I loved her, said "See you in Heaven," and walked out of the room.

I met Mark in the hall. We walked up the hall past the other rooms through the double wooden doors in silence. Then Mark said, "What just happened"?

"I don't know," I replied. "This all seems like a very bad dream." I felt pain, disbelief, anger, cheated—so many emotions flooding me at one time. I would never see my best friend, lover, soul mate again. I felt like I was leaving her. I was so helpless.

We kept walking. Mark and I talked a little bit, both shocked and in disbelief that we were leaving Connie. So many times she had beaten cancer. Now we were walking away without her.

At some point, Mark asked where I had parked. I thought about it for a moment. "I don't remember," I said. I had arrived at the hospital approximately forty-eight hours earlier. Mark said, "We'll drive around and find your car." The hospital has a parking garage, a parking lot for the ER, and one in front of the outpatients' entrance. At one time or another, I had parked in all of them.

We put Connie's belongings in the back seat of Mark's truck and started to search for my car. I was totally numb and could not think. I could cry at the drop of a bucket, shattered. We drove through the parking garage and finally spotted my car. I asked Mark, "Can you please follow me home to make sure I get there?" I got out of the truck, opened the car, and started to drive. I tried to keep Mark in my rearview mirror. Neither of us was in very good shape. We should not have been driving alone. Everyone else had someone in the car for the trip home.

It had rained earlier that night, the roads were wet, and it was really foggy. Between my tears and the fog, I could not see the road at times. My emotions were all over the place. No understanding, my life was pure chaos. To this day, I do not know how I made it home. The only thing I know it had to be God and His angels who helped me get there. Finally, the driveway and the house, I was home.

Mark wanted to come in. We unloaded Connie's belongings, dropped everything in the dining room, and went into the living room. I sat on the couch and Mark sat on the love seat. It was July and I was very cold; I took the comforter and wrapped up in it.

Mark and I talked for a little while about what had just happened. The hardest part was walking down the hall and leaving. I was so tired, as I had only had a few hours of sleep in the last 48 hours and that was catching up with me. I fell asleep on Mark. He woke me up and said he was leaving. I told him to sleep on the couch, but he wanted to go home. Mark left. I walked into the bedroom, crawled into bed, and fell asleep.

Ring, ring, ring; it was the telephone by my bed. I heard it but could not react quickly enough. The answering machine picked up and went through the greeting. "Mr. Sabo, this is Sam from the funeral home. Please call me as soon as you get this message." He left his phone number.

Yeah, right, I thought. I looked at the alarm next to the phone, 7:00 a.m. Wow, almost two hours of sleep. I'll call him later. At least when I sleep, I do not think. A half hour later, the same thing happened. Now I was getting somewhat angry. I lay there for a little bit to wake up.

I didn't want to deal with it, but I called Sam back. It turned out that they needed my authorization to pick up Connie. I hung up the phone and rolled over to go back to sleep.

An hour later, the phone rang again. I couldn't believe it. This time it was Debbie, the HR from work, wanting to know when I was coming back to work.

I had missed the last few days of work and it was the end of the pay period. I filled out the paperwork for me to go on FMLA, which protects your job so you won't lose it for missing too much work. If you are ever in a situation like this, please do FMLA. I heard the message and would call her later. They did not know yet that Connie had passed away. I tried to go back to sleep, but this time it was not going to happen.

I got up but did not know what to do. Okay, think what you normally do. I made my way to the kitchen and poured myself some orange juice. I grabbed the phone and went to sit on the couch. I drank some OJ and stared into space.

I called work and asked for Debbie in HR. She answered the phone in her upbeat voice. "Hey, Gabe, I wanted to touch base with you and see how things were going and when you think you might be back to work." I said, "I don't know. Connie passed away last night." As I write this, I did not want to be so blunt about it. It was the mood I was in. There was total silence on the other end. After an awkward silence, she said, "Gabe, I am so sorry. I didn't know. If I had known, I wouldn't have called so early." I finally snapped back into reality and had a conversation with her. I would let her know the arrangements when they were made. I hung up the phone. I was so cold and hungry. I was freezing and it was July in PA. It was not cold out, seventy-five degrees or so.

I was numb. I just stared out the glass door into the backyard. The emptiness, loneliness, hurt, anger, and again the ocean of tears. I did not know what to do. "God, please help me." I was angry with Him, but I needed His help.

I sat on the couch, my knees against my chest, my arms wrapped around my legs, with a red throw that was on the couch I used to drape around my shoulders. "God, what do I do?" My next thought was to call Mom. I picked up my cell phone, found Mom's phone number, and called. After a few rings, she answered. All I could say was "Mom, what do I do now?"

*   *   *   *

Life is all about choices we make. I could have chosen not to go to Mark's house with Connie, but with what I know now, I am so thankful that I made the right choice by working on the house with her. It was not until Connie left this life to dance her way across Heaven that I discovered how important the choices were and I do not regret them at all. Mark and I have talked many times about the memories we have from working on his house and glad that we took the time to make them. Some people are so busy with life that they do not make wise choices in spending time with family and then that person is gone and they wished they had spent more time with them.

I moved from Pennsylvania to Waynesboro, Virginia, in April 2012. I have kept in contact with Connie's family either by phone, email, or text. I did not talk to Mark for a while. There were no issues, just life. Mark works different shifts and it is difficult to connect due to his work schedule. He works days then switches over to midnights, so it's hard to know when to call. We send a few texts back and forth to keep in touch. About the middle of November 2012, I got a text from Mark at 8:30 in the morning stating that he had moved into his house. That made me very excited. I tried to call him, but the cell phone was acting up so we did not have a good connection. Therefore, we went to texting, and in the conversation I could tell how excited he was to be in the house. I don't know how long we texted back and forth. At one point, I had a thought; I knew it had to be a God thought. The thought was that not very many people can move into a new house for the first time and move in already having created memories in that house.

My mind raced from thought after thought to the many years of working on his house and especially the six or seven months that Connie and I got to help him before she passed away. I texted him that he moved into the house already having memories. I could tell that this took him by surprise because it took him a few minutes to reply and then he said he agreed.

That is just like God to arrange something like that. I know how much it meant to Mark to have Connie and me help him on the house and for him that was priceless. Folks, one thing I've learned in all this is that life is about building good memories. Please take the time to create good memories. You will never regret it.

ACKNOWLEDGMENTS

THIS BOOK HAS TAKEN me over nine years to write. There were so many people who helped and encouraged me along the way—thank you! There were so many times it seemed that I would never get through it, but I did. My editor, Stephanie Marohn, thank you for helping me out in bringing this book to life. Thanks to the talented cover designer Marrianne Russell who illustrated my vision beautifully. I would like to thank everyone personally, but there are so many people, from family and friends to coworkers, that I would to have another chapter just with all of your names. You know who you are. I want to thank you from the depths of my heart for all you have done; you are amazing people. Without all your love and support this book would not have been completed. It is my prayer that each of you will be blessed because of it.

And to all of you out there who have read this book, thank you for taking the time to read it and to join me on my journey through cancer. My prayer is that, in some way, I was able to inspire, help, or encourage you. If you are a caregiver, going through cancer, or helping someone that is, what you have read will give you what you need to get to the finish line. You have listened to me talk about my faith throughout this book. I can tell you, I would not have made it if I did not have God. Thank you again for reading my book.

—Gabe

When writing this book, a few chapters were handwritten by me. I was visiting my mom at the time. She had a few physical issues in addition to losing my dad about two years prior to this visit. I asked her if she'd help me by typing these chapters into the computer. She had already begun typing when she took a break and then wrote this. I almost entitled this book, Life is Like a Hurricane. This part was written by my mom who was seventy eight at the time. I wanted this left unedited so it would reflect the way she wrote it. Enjoy.

Life is Like a Hurricane

The sun is shining, the sky is blue, birds are singing. Life is good, all is well. Suddenly there are clouds on the horizon! Along comes a hurricane! We are pounded, bruised, tossed around in the storm. Life changes there are problems loss of work, financial problems and sickness. It is so dark we can't see any hope. GOD where are you! I need you. The storm keeps on.

Then the storm slows and the sun is shining, the sky is blue, birds are singing. We are in the eye of the hurricane. It is calm and peaceful. Life is good again. Oh no here comes the back side of the hurricane!

The back side is stronger, more powerful. Once again we are pounded, bruised, more sickness we are tossed about like a feather in the wind. This time the storm is more powerful, more destructive GOD I can't find you! Where are you? It is so dark. I need your help. When will this storm end? How much sorrow can I endure? I feel so lost.

The storm dies down, the sun comes out, the sky is blue, the birds are singing again. God says I was with you all through the storm, the trials, testing, sickness, and the death of your loved ones. I never left you. I felt your pain and sorrow. Look around and see a new day I have for you.

By Peggy Sabo